THE PATRIARCA
MAFIA CRIME FAMILY

The Complete History of a New England Criminal Organization

MAFIA LIBRARY

© **Copyright 2023 - All rights reserved.**

The content contained within this book may not be reproduced, duplicated or transmitted without direct written permission from the author or the publisher.

Under no circumstances will any blame or legal responsibility be held against the publisher, or author, for any damages, reparation, or monetary loss due to the information contained within this book, either directly or indirectly.

Legal Notice:

This book is copyright protected. It is only for personal use. You cannot amend, distribute, sell, use, quote or paraphrase any part, or the content within this book, without the consent of the author or publisher.

Disclaimer Notice:

Please note the information contained within this document is for educational and entertainment purposes only. All effort has been executed to present accurate, up to date, reliable, complete information. No warranties of any kind are declared or implied. Readers acknowledge that the author is not engaged in the rendering of legal, financial, medical or professional advice. The content within this book has been derived from various sources. Please consult a licensed professional before attempting any techniques outlined in this book.

By reading this document, the reader agrees that under no circumstances is the author responsible for any losses, direct or indirect, that are incurred as a result of the use of the information contained within this document, including, but not limited to, errors, omissions, or inaccuracies.

TABLE OF CONTENTS

Introduction 1

Chapter 1 : The Godfathers Of New England 7
   Prohibition And The Castellammarese War 8
   One Family 16

Chapter 2 : The Rise Of Raymond Patriarca 23
   "I Guess I Drifted A Little…" 24
   Il Patrone, A Made Guy 27

Chapter 3 : The Patriarca Crime Family 37
   The New Providence Regime 38
   The Witness You Can't Kill 45

Chapter 4 : The 1970s, From Behind Bars 57
   Facing Kennedy's Music 58
   Patriarca Returns 63

Chapter 5 : Junior Takes The Reins 69
   Gone For Good 70
   Junior's Downfall 73

Chapter 6 : Discontent In The Commonwealth 79
   Junior's Last Straw 80
   The Troublesome 90s 84

Chapter 7 : Collapse: The Mafia Today 89
    Salemme And The Civil War 90
    The Patriarcas In The 21st Century 92

Conclusion 101

References 107

INTRODUCTION

One evening, in late September of 1916, a husband and wife were walking back to their home in the Boston suburb of Brookline, Massachusetts. A respected member of the community, the man would have been easily recognizable around town. He had been successfully operating a produce importing company in the city and had important political connections both in Boston and in his native hometown in Sicily, where his ships loaded tons of fruit destined for the Boston Harbor. His name carried a lot of weight, particularly in the Italian neighborhoods of urban Massachusetts. Specializing in citrus fruits, he was fondly nicknamed "The Lemon King." His real name was Gaspare DiCola, and the woman he was walking home with that evening was Antonina, his wife (although it seems that the pair were never officially married). The couple certainly wasn't looking for trouble that night—Gaspare was 50 years old in 1916 and Antonina was just a few months behind him. They were unassuming, and looking forward to a peaceful night at home. But, before they could reach their house on Fairbanks Street, two unseen figures approached the DiColas from behind and shot five rounds from their pistols into Gaspare before fleeing the scene.

Gaspare and Antonina were returning from the local Massachusetts Dante Alighieri Society, an organization founded back in 1889 to promote the culture and language of Italy abroad, especially in Italian diaspora communities. Gaspare, who had emigrated from his hometown in Palermo, Sicily to the United States sometime between the late 1880s and early 1890s, clearly had pride for his Italian roots even after he became a naturalized U.S. citizen around 1896 at a ceremony in Boston. Still, America was his home, and he had already made a name for himself in the 20-odd years since he first stepped onto American shores. His importing headquarters on Boston's North End waterfront was well-known, and since 1911 he had served on Boston's Board of Children's Institutions and Services, a position he had been personally appointed to by the city's Mayor, John F. Fitzgerald (who happened to be the grandfather of future U.S. President John F. Kennedy). He was even President of the Boston chapter of the Italian Red Cross committee, an international humanitarian group. There is no obvious reason that someone would have wanted this high-profile member of the community gunned down in the street, but it has long been suspected that Gaspare DiCola was, in fact, the boss of a New England Mafia Family.

In 1916, the Mafia was a concept about which the public knew very little. Many who lived in the communities in which the Mafia operated had a general notion that there was *something* connecting the seemingly organized criminal activity in the major cities across the United States, but it would be nearly half a century before an actual member of *La Cosa Nostra* (literally meaning "our thing," or "this thing of ours") would publicly admit that the Mafia existed and had a national structure. After all, one of the central tenets of the Italian-American Mafia was *omerta*, an oath of silence that forbade its members from speaking about the "business" to anyone who was not a member, especially law enforcement, a rule that went almost completely unbroken for decades.

Still, there are a few major reasons to suspect that DiCola was one of those prominent and upstanding citizens who liked to make a living on the side, in Boston's criminal underworld. First and most obviously, Gaspare's shooting was certainly not random. His assailants took no chances and got close enough to their target to identify him before shooting. The shooting was clearly planned—someone wanted Gaspare DiCola dead. Second, as the 50-year-old lay in his hospital bed in Boston, in critical condition, he refused to cooperate with Boston police in any way. If he spoke to them at all, it was to reassure them that somehow neither Gaspare nor his wife could recall a single identifying detail about their attackers. This is a major red flag, as in these early days the sense of duty that bound mafiosi to *omerta* was strong, and it was taboo to work with the police even if it was against your enemies or killers. In the Mafia world, disputes were settled amongst themselves, not outsiders. Lastly, and perhaps most striking, the eventual death of Gaspare from his injuries the next morning was followed shortly after by the rise of another bona fide Mafia boss in Boston: Gaspare Messina. If DiCola's death created a void in the criminal underworld leadership, it had now been filled.

DiCola's story—at its base—is not unique, though it is one of the earliest in New England's history. More or less the same tale would play out again and again over the next hundred years in major cities across the country. A mafioso begins building an empire for himself by creating connections and a base of power until eventually his enemies (or sometimes, his friends) decide that he has gotten too greedy. He's taken out, replaced by another "made" guy, and the cycle repeats until he's either killed or put in prison. In New York, Boston, Chicago, Philadelphia, Los Angeles, and elsewhere, the history of the Italian-American Mafia is written in blood and betrayal. Although Mafia bosses have generally been considered untouchable for most of the Mafia's history, greed and selfishness slowly eroded what made the organization successful. But, although the Mafia in the 21st century is a shell of its former self, it has proven incredibly resilient in the face of decades of infighting and aggressive legal prosecution. Many Mafia families are still active today in whatever illicit markets they can penetrate, and the vast majority of them can—in one way or another—trace their lineage back to New York City; the national hub of Mafia activity in America. Even the Rizzuto Family of Montreal, Canada began as an extension of the Bonanno Family, one of New York City's infamous "Five Families." The Mafia in New England was no exception.

American port cities at the beginning of the 20th century were lands of immigrants. As the underclass of Europe sought better lives for themselves and their families, they poured in on immigrant ships through coastal cities like Boston, New Orleans, and especially New York. Though America is a melting pot of cultures, these men and women invariably brought their own culture and values with them to their new homes. Sicily and the southern Italian mainland (where the Mafia first began) was a major source of immigrants to America in the 20th century, and so many people were coming in that, inevitably, some had been connected to the Sicilian Mafia. Most newly arrived immigrants tended to make their homes in communities where their fellow immigrants lived, resulting in close-knit enclaves—Italians with Italians, Irish with Irish, Chinese with Chinese, etc.—allowing their shared culture to grow and flourish. Complicating matters was the fact that these immigrants were often discriminated against and had no hope of securing anything other than the lowest-paid, most dangerous jobs. As a result, the Mafia was eventually reborn in America, most powerfully in New York City. Here, five large families came to dominate the city's criminal ecosystem, and the oldest of these, the Genovese

Family, traces its heritage all the way back to Giuseppe Morello, one of the earliest-known mobsters who began his first gang in the 1890s. From this nucleus, the Mafia grew and took root in other cities. Importantly for our story, Boston, Massachusetts, and Providence, Rhode Island were two of these cities.

Regardless of what region they controlled, Mafia Families tended to follow a similar structure. At the bottom of the hierarchy were the "associates," the non-members who were still valuable to the Mafia and were known to work with them. Sometimes associates were those who simply hadn't been "made" yet, sometimes they were unable to ever be "made" because they were non-Sicilian (or non-Italian). Regardless, associates were typically organized into crews run by soldiers, who occupied the lowest rank of the "made" men. Associates helped organize heists and run the Mafia's several criminal operations. Whatever they made, they kicked up a portion to soldiers, who in turn kicked up to the Family's *caporegimes*, otherwise known as captains. *Capos* acted as a kind of middle management for the Mafia, overseeing larger operations and running their own crews which consisted of lower-ranking members. They earned more money and had plenty of people paying them, but they also had to kick up to the boss (the man in charge of the entire Family and its operations) and their second-in-command, the Family's underboss. In the early years of the Mafia in New England, after the death of Gaspare DiCola and before the factions were organized into a single Family unit, there were two bosses trying to build crime empires: Messina in Boston, and later, Frank Morelli in Providence.

Messina and Morelli built their own crews independently, but their respective cities eventually became two centers of a united organization that spanned across several northeastern states at the height of its power. In this region, huge portions of all criminal activity—from union racketeering to paid assassinations—were monopolized by the New England Mafia for decades. During the 1920s, the power of both the Boston and Providence crews grew even more as a result of the federal prohibition on alcohol that began in 1920 and lasted for 13 years. Those in the criminal underworld were presented with a lucrative opportunity to keep the booze flowing through the streets of America's cities, and this period began the criminal careers of many infamous gangsters, including Al Capone and Charles "Lucky" Luciano, to name a few. The new source of wealth that came with bootleg alcohol production and rum running sustained the more successful Families for years, and they could now purchase more political connections than ever before. After much infighting and bloodshed through the early 1930s, the national Mafia was consolidated and became even stronger as a result of the Castellammarese War and the creation of "The Commission."

The Commission was the brainchild of Lucky Luciano and was his attempt at making the national organization more centralized, cohesive, and even democratic. It brought together the most powerful and respected Mafia bosses from across America's cities with a simple mandate; to govern national Mafia activities and to serve as an arbiter for disputes which, in prior decades, had torn Families apart from within. Along with the forming of the Commission came a major restructuring of the American Mafia as a whole, which had huge implications for New England's disconnected and fragmented criminal underworld in the 1930s. The organization that would eventually become known as the Patriarca Crime Family first coalesced in this period, and these early years will be the focus of our first chapter.

CHAPTER 1

THE GODFATHERS OF NEW ENGLAND

Long before the legendary Raymond Loreda Salvatore Patriarca stepped into the commanding role of a united New England organization, the Mafia's presence and power in Massachusetts, Rhode Island, Connecticut, and elsewhere were relatively weak. Further, they were plagued by frequent wars with other ethnic gangs in the city, most notably with Boston's Irish Mob. It would take a few decades before the Sicilian-American Mafia in New England would come to rival the power of their counterpart Families in New York City, but the activities of the two regions were highly connected during this time, and events in NYC would forever change the landscape of crime along America's northeast seaboard. Messina had strong Mafia ties to New York, which proved invaluable during Prohibition and helped to grow the influence of the faction in Boston; the city that became the headquarters of the Family until Patriarca took over operations in the 1950s. Messina also personally had an important role to play during the Castellammarese War in NYC. His counterpart in Providence, Frank Morelli, had a much more modest role and power base, but as we'll see, the Rhode Island faction also underwent some drastic changes in these early decades.

Prohibition and the Castellammarese War

Prior to approximately the late 1940s and early 1950s, relatively little is known about the inner workings and finer details of the New England Mafia, at least in comparison to the Five Families of New York. There is, however, much speculation and conflicting stories about these years, as is the case with the circumstances of Gaspare DiCola's death. Despite so many signs pointing toward DiCola being one of Boston's first crime bosses, there exists little to no actual evidence from the time linking him to the city's rackets and other known criminals. Yet, his role as one of New England's earliest "Godfathers" has nevertheless made its way into the region's Mafia lore. Whatever events preceded DiCola's murder, we do know that Gaspare Messina was the new big man in Boston after 1916. Again though, Messina is a character about whom we know frustratingly little for certain.

What we do know about him is that, like DiCola and many other early mafiosi, Messina was born in southern Italy in the town of Salemi, an inland commune of western Sicily. About 13 years DiCola's junior, Messina left his southern Italian home and immigrated to the United States sometime around 1905. His was one of many immigrant ships destined for the harbors of New York City (specifically, Messina with his wife and brother landed on the famous Ellis Island), and it was here that Messina made his first American home. He began to build a life for himself and soon settled down in Brooklyn, where he would remain for about a decade. He made an honest living to support his family, opening up a neighborhood bakery in Brooklyn that he ran with his family. Before long though, Gaspare was supplementing his salary with more illicit income. It's unclear when, but at some point during his early years in New York City, Gaspare Messina had joined the Mafia. He was the newest member of the Bonanno Crime Family.

Messina would retain life-long business and personal connections to New York, but he was not destined to remain in the city forever. By 1915, he and his family had relocated to the major New England city of Boston, Massachusetts (some sources claim the move wasn't made until later in the decade). Boston was another popular immigrant city at the time and had a healthy population of Italians, but in Boston, the Irish healthily outnumbered the Italians. The result was higher competition between ethnic gangs over resources and criminal rackets, which often boiled over into gang wars. When Messina first moved to the area though, the Mafia there often had more to fear from their own people rather than outsiders. Coincidence or not, within just one year of Messina's arrival in Boston, Gaspare DiCola would be brutally and publicly murdered on his own neighborhood streets. Not long after DiCola's death, Messina began seizing much of the criminal operations throughout Boston's North End, particularly gambling, counterfeiting, and a few years later, bootlegging. Unfortunately for Messina, it's unwise to live lavishly with no way to explain to the government how you earned all of your money, and so he reopened his old family bakery in his new home to serve as one of his several "front" businesses (essentially, fronts were establishments designed to give the appearance of legitimate and legal income—profits from criminal activities could be reported to the Internal Revenue Service as income generated from legal business, thus cleaning or "laundering" the money).

The exact circumstances and rationale surrounding Messina's arrival in Boston are, for the most part, unknown. It's possible that he decided to relocate purely of his own volition, seeking out a smaller city where he could more easily carve out a place for himself to operate. It's possible, though unlikely, that Messina was fleeing New York due to either safety concerns or pending legal investigation. What's more likely though is that Messina was asked to make the move by the leadership of the New York Families. It was not uncommon for the most powerful organizations to send their own men to other cities in order for the Family to both gain a foothold in and oversee the area's racket operations. Messina was probably sent to New England as a *rappresentante*, or "representative" of the national Boss of Bosses, known in Italian as the *capo di tutti capi*. Prior to the creation of the Mafia Commission, the Boss of Bosses was a title typically given to the most powerful and respected boss of the New York Families. At the time Messina left New York for Boston, that man would have been Salvatore D'Aquila, boss of the organization that would become known as the Gambino Crime Family. Having a made guy like Messina in another city to represent both the interests of the Bonannos as well as D'Aquila would not have been unusual. Of course, it would have also been a very lucrative opportunity for Messina himself.

Whatever the reason for his entrance into Boston's North End, Messina quickly set to work intimidating and extorting his way to a commanding position within Boston's underworld. The remainder of the decade was spent pursuing this goal, but the 1920s soon brought a new, incredibly profitable source of income for those willing (and able) to break the rules. In 1919, the Protestant Christian groups in the United States that had long been calling for an end to the sale and production of alcohol, including the Women's Christian Temperance Union, finally succeeded on a congressional level. These groups blamed everything from family violence to political corruption on the scourge of alcohol, and

Congress finally gave in to pressure with the ratification of the 18th Amendment. No longer could American citizens legally purchase liquor, outside of religious purposes. The problem was that Americans still very much enjoyed alcohol and were not willing to give it up. And so, the underground black market for beer and liquor became big business, especially for the Mafia.

In major cities across the country, various Mafia Families came to dominate the bootlegging markets, and Boston was no different. The city was a big market and Messina ensured a steady flow of bootleg liquor through its North End districts. It was apparently so profitable that he and his associates needed new streams of legitimate revenue. To that end, Messina established sometime in the early 1920s the Messina & Company Grocery on Prince Street. His partners in this venture were two of his associates, Paolo Pagnotta and Frank Cucchiara. Pagnotta had to leave the partnership before long due to his publicized 1925 arrest, along with two of his associates who ended up receiving charges for carrying concealed handguns. These early years also were not *entirely* kind to Messina either. In 1923 he became the suspect in a large investigation into approximately $500,000 USD in counterfeit bills flooding Boston's economy. Not much appears to have come of it, but it seems very likely that the investigators were looking into the right person. Messina was known to have a hand in the counterfeiting business, and aside from that, he mysteriously vanished from the state once the investigation picked up steam. He had gone back to his native Sicily before returning stateside in late 1924.

When Messina arrived back in Boston, he was facing exactly zero criminal charges relating to his counterfeiting operation. Still, by the middle of the decade, life as the top criminal in Boston had taken its toll on the boss, and the stress was beginning to affect his health. He decided to step down as boss of the Boston faction based out of the North End. In future decades, the Mafia Commission would have stepped in to handle a situation like this, convening and ultimately voting to select and confirm a new boss to fill the void. In the 1920s though, no such apparatus existed and when it came to disputes, it was the Wild West. Messina's absence led to a power struggle in the region for control over the businesses and rackets that were formerly his domain. The North End's illegal gambling clubs and card games, loan sharking, and the highly lucrative bootlegging were all up for grabs. Fighting ensued, but ultimately it was the gangster from east Boston Filippo (Phil) Buccola who rose above the rest and inherited the commanding share of Messina's fledgling empire. He then set to work consolidating and reorganizing the fractured criminal world Messina left behind. Unfortunately for some, this included going to war with the city's other gangs.

One of the biggest rivals to Buccola's faction of the Mafia was operating out of South Boston, a neighborhood familiarly known as "Southie." In this part of the city, it was the Irish gangs that ruled. Of these, it was the Gustin Gang, run by the Irish Wallace brothers, that posed the most serious competition for Boston's underworld. The Wallace brothers earned their early reputation mostly with robberies and hijackings (the eldest, Frank, was involved in a high-profile case in Detroit where he had been accused of robbery of over $10,000, but he and his brothers had a lot of important friends and none of the charges ended up sticking to Frank). When Prohibition hit, the Wallaces found a new way to profit from their illegal hobby—they began tracking and hijacking the trucks belonging to rival bootlegging gangs and stealing their shipments of liquor. This was clever, as criminals have little recourse when they themselves are victimized, and the Bureau of Prohibition was not in the business of helping bootleggers recover their stolen, illegal whiskey. Further, the Wallaces were known to dress up as law enforcement when they raided their rivals, complete with police-style weapons and fake badges, so oftentimes they would simply assume that the law had confiscated their product, meanwhile the Gustin Gang was reselling the contraband to other establishments. Among the many smuggling trucks that the Wallaces hit throughout the 1920s, several of them belonged to the Italians—it's no surprise that this manner of hit-and-run thievery did not sit well with Buccola's Family on the north side of the city.

Instrumental in Buccola's war against the Irish rum-jackers was his underboss, Joseph Lombardo (sometimes Lombardo is referred to as his *consigliere*, a kind of close personal advisor to a boss—it's possible that he held both roles at different times, or simultaneously). Born sometime in the late 1890s, Lombardo was another native of Salemi, Sicily, and as such he carried similar "Old World" values. During his time in Mafia leadership, Lombardo became a very highly respected elder statesman kind of figure both regionally in Massachusetts and at a national underworld level. He was known to be diplomatic and was often consulted as an arbiter in gangland disputes, but ironically, he is easily best known for his role in orchestrating a double homicide (although it was his goal to murder three that day). As a result of the Gustin Gang's repeated hits on Buccola's trucks (including the most recent hijacking in which the North End mob lost approximately $50,000 in merchandise to the Irish), Lombardo called a meeting with Frank and his top guys just a few days before Christmas, 1931, to discuss a resolution. The Wallaces were no fools and they expected a backstab, so when Frank showed up at Lombardo's office building, he, Tim Coffey, and "Dodo" Walsh were all armed to the teeth. Still, it was Lombardo who got the drop on them. As the Irish gangsters waited for Buccola's underboss to usher them into his office, a hail of bullets blasted through closed doors and cut down both Frank and Dodo. Coffey was luckier and managed to hide before he caught a bullet.

With Frank out of the picture, his younger brother Steve Wallace came to head the now-emaciated Gustin Gang. It soon became obvious to their rivals that Frank was the true power in the gang, and Steve was never able to recover the influence that his brother had garnered for their family. It's unclear what the role of James, the youngest brother, was exactly, but his presence was evidently not too beneficial. The market formerly controlled by the Irish out of Southie was now up for the taking by Buccola and Lombardo. Unfortunately for them and other bootleggers, the 18th Amendment was not long for this world in 1931. The entrance of organized crime into the bootleg liquor business caused years of gang violence and public bloodbaths in the streets of cities across the country. To make matters worse, Prohibition simply wasn't working. Bootleggers, and especially the Mafia, had become so adept at eluding law enforcement that just about anyone who wanted booze would be able to get it. By 1933, the once powerful and vocal support for Prohibition had diminished to a whisper.

The 21st Amendment officially repealed Prohibition, and gangsters everywhere lost the most valuable source of income they had yet known. Still, the profits generated from the 13 years of bootlegging built the legacies of mobsters that would last for decades. Gaspare Messina had profited handsomely while he sat atop Boston's gangster totem pole, and even though he had assumed a background role by the late 1920s, he had created quite a life for himself. Around the late 1920s and early 1930s, he became president of Neptune Oil, his own petrol company based out of the Boston harbor. Buccola too had built himself an empire that would sustain him over 20 years later. But the bosses weren't the only ones making big moves during Prohibition. In the nearby Rhode Island city of Providence, where the Mafia faction was even weaker, a young small-time thug named Raymond Patriarca was cutting his teeth hijacking liquor trucks and running them out of state. A protege of the powerful Don Iacone who operated out of Worcester, MA, and Providence, Patriarca would soon become a pivotal figure in the history of the New England Mafia.

It seems that by 1932, Gaspare Messina, one of the Godfathers of New England, was fully out of Mafia life. After he had stepped down as the boss in Boston, he was called on once more around 1931-32 to serve the Mafia at a national level. His reputation and the respect he commanded were valuable during this time, as the New York-based Families were embroiled in a massive conflict that came to be known as the Castellammarese War. With the rise in power and status of the American Mafia, the old Families back home in Sicily decided to make a play for control of U.S. territory from their immigrant cousins across the Atlantic. The Sicilian faction from the coastal Castellammare Del Golfo region of the island had sent representatives to New York to try to wrest control away from the Families who at the time were headed by *capo di tutti capi* Giuseppe Masseria, also known as Joe the Boss. The Castellammarese faction was headed by the Sicilian lieutenant Salvatore Maranzano, who was representing the interests of his boss in Italy. For a brief period during the turmoil caused by the war, it was Gaspare Messina who was selected to serve as "boss of bosses," likely in the immediate aftermath of Joe Masseria's murder. Messina was likely living in New York City at the time, and so his role here didn't directly affect the New England Families, but as we'll see, the events following Maranzano's victory in the Castellammarese War had massive implications for both Buccola in Boston and Frank Morelli in Providence.

One Family

In the immediate aftermath of the war in New York City, the Mafia's presence in New England was still fractured, and Buccola and Morelli each ran their own separate operations. Buccola, who had only been in America since about 1920, had first begun earning income by managing professional boxers and prizefighters. He partnered in this with an associate based in New York, the city where Buccola had initially entered the U.S. Born in 1886, Buccola was already in his thirties when he immigrated out of Sicily but he wasted no time entering the criminal underworld once he was there, which suggests that he very likely was already a made member of a Family in Sicily when he left. When he eventually made his way to Boston, he initially set up his base of operation in the East Side of the city where he grew his power during Prohibition until he came to replace Messina as Boston's kingpin.

In 1932 when Messina permanently retired, Buccola was recognized by the New York Families as his legitimate successor. However, according to Mafia turncoat Vincent Teresa, Buccola was being used as a front man by the true Boston don, Joe Lombardo, sometimes known as Big Joe L. There's not much besides Teresa's word that substantiates the claim that Lombardo was the man behind the curtain, and all signs point to Buccola instead. During the 20s and early 30s, Buccola was still, for the most part, sharing the wealth, especially with "King" Solomon, a Jewish gangster from the West End who was heavily active in the city's rum-running operations. After Buccola became boss though, this arrangement didn't last.

Solomon was a true founding father of organized crime in New England and had made a fortune peddling narcotics even before Prohibition began. He was influential too, holding sway in New York among the Mafia intelligentsia and elder statesmen, and his nature of arbitrating disputes supposedly influenced the creation of the so-called National Crime Syndicate coalition. At the beginning of 1933, his time was up. After a long night at Boston's Coconut Grove nightclub, which was a notorious hotspot for organized criminals between 1927 and 1942, Solomon and his entourage of women made for the Cotton Club in the South End. After a while at their new location, Solomon at some point stood up and went to the bathroom before being followed by two men sitting at a nearby table. There was muffled gunfire followed by screaming before the two men ran out of the bathroom and fled the club. A few moments later, a severely injured Solomon staggered out, covered in blood, and collapsed. He had been hit several times in the neck and torso at close range, and he died soon after. Neither of the gunmen, John Burke or Jimmy Coyne, were Sicilians, but it has long been understood that Philip Buccola was the man who orchestrated and authorized the killing. Buccola doesn't appear to have made a play for the Jewish kingpin's former territory, but his faction was significantly weakened.

This was Buccola's Boston in the early 1930s. In Rhode Island, criminal operations were organizing themselves and becoming more centralized, but Providence's Frank Morelli was an entirely different breed from his Boston counterpart. For starters, he wasn't an immigrant like the majority of his colleagues at the time. It was for a long time assumed that Morelli had come from the Foggia region of southern Italy in the late 1890s, but evidence suggests that his parents made the move to America long before he was born—Morelli (originally spelled Molarelli, and Frank's given name was Adolfo) was born, and died, in Providence. He and his brothers (he was the youngest of five) seem to have begun their criminal careers in the 1910s, when Frank, who was born in 1896, was still young. The eldest brother, Joe, had started a loosely organized gang of neighborhood youths after the passing of their father Gennaro, which included several, if not all, of his brothers. The gang was petty at first, committing nighttime burglaries and theft, but they eventually graduated to far more brazen robberies. Their favorite targets ended up being large freights, which were profitable when successful, but they also brought more serious charges. Given that the cargo was often bound for out-of-state cities, robbing them would have been considered an interstate crime, and thus would carry federal punishments. The brothers' recklessness soon caught up with them.

In 1919, an investigation into the hijacking of a large shipment of shoes from a transport train led to the arrest of a number of Morelli gang members, including the leader Joe. Another wave of arrests hit the gang soon after, this time for the robbery of a truck carrying the payroll of a local shoe factory. Rhode Island police had suspected that the two crimes were linked, and so the Morellis were under investigation once again. Frank got picked up by police and was convicted in 1920, but this was getting off very easy in comparison to two of his fellow gang members. Complicating the payroll heist case was the fact that, in the course of the crime, someone from the Morelli gang (or all of them) decided that witnesses couldn't be tolerated, and so the drivers of the truck were shot dead. Law enforcement decided that this warranted making an example of the Providence gangs, and so they made their case and pursued it aggressively. Their selected villains were gang associates Nicola Sacco and Bartolomeo Vanzetti. Court proceedings were hotly contested and six years passed before a final verdict was rendered. The court eventually determined that Sacco and Vanzetti were the chief victimizers in the robbery, and their sentence was the electric chair. In the summer of 1927, the two men were executed by the state for double homicide.

Frank himself was out of his Atlanta prison cell by the end of February 1924, and the world he was re-entering was already steeped in Prohibition-era bootlegging. Relocating back home to Providence, Morelli quickly proved that the American justice system of the early 20th century was less than effective. He was rearrested just months later for armed assault, and his violent incidents would continue for years. Some of his brothers appear to have still been committed to their robberies and hijackings, but Frank had bigger things in mind when he went back to Rhode Island. He began a bloody turf war in Providence in an attempt to seize control of the majority of the city's rackets. His main games appear to have been Prohibition, but especially gambling. Just like his young self, his crimes were brazen. Once again there is little evidence, but Frank is generally considered the man who organized the 1931 bombing of the home of a notorious Providence gangster who oversaw much of the illegal gambling in the city. His luck wasn't over quite yet though, and he escaped that investigation with nothing but suspicion. In less than five years after his former co-conspirators were put to death, Frank had taken over much of

Providence's racketeering and he had become a pioneer of the Mafia in Rhode Island.

So, in the early 1930s, things in Boston and Providence were developing nicely for their respective bosses. But, just as operations were becoming more steady and consolidated across the two states, they were about to be shaken up again. After the Castellammarese War, the Mafia landscape was altered everywhere. Charles "Lucky" Luciano, the New York boss who was pivotal in ending the war in 1931, had petitioned the Mafia community to create the Mafia Commission. Luciano had seen firsthand the kind of mutual destruction that came as a result of all-out turf wars, namely loss of profit, and the Commission was his solution—the mandate of those serving on the Commission (which would consist of the most respected bosses across the nation) was to intervene in, mediate, and settle high-profile gangland disputes before they could ever evolve into another Castellammarese War. This was meant to be in the best interest of the entire national Mafia. But if this was to be possible, the Mafia needed to be more centralized and there needed to be more authority vested in a smaller group of powerful men. This applied across the country. In New York City, the Five Families-style organization was officially implemented to contain competition in the massive city. In New England, it was decided that neither Boston nor Providence, the two main hubs for Mafia activity in the region, were large enough to justify having separate Commission-approved Families and bosses. The national leaders insisted that the two factions be merged under a single Family banner.

The question still remained: Which boss would receive the blessing of the newly-created Commission? Which city would become the new nexus of crime in New England? The obvious choice was

Buccola's faction in Boston. His city was a much larger market than Providence, and the Mafia's presence there was already more substantial and growing faster. On top of this, Buccola was Sicilian-born like much of the old leadership in NYC and elsewhere, plus Morelli's history with violence and run-ins with the law were considered potential liabilities for a regional boss. The only negative was that despite the best efforts of Buccola and his predecessors, the Irish still outnumbered Italians in Boston, and Irish gangs still posed a considerable threat to Mafia operations. Nevertheless, Morelli was passed over for the position of boss. Given Morelli's reputation, it's possible that this could have evolved into a war over the position of New England boss but as the story goes, it was Joe Lombardo who apparently visited Morelli and convinced him to accept the determination of the Commission and to take himself out of the running. It's also possible that Morelli was simply bowing to more experienced leadership. In any case, New England was now set to face the rest of the 1930s under a united Mafia Family led by Philip Buccola and Joe Lombardo out of Boston. Frank Morelli still remained the top man in Providence, but he now had his own boss to answer to. Until 1954 when he finally retired, that man was Buccola.

The Gustin Gang was destroyed, Charles "King" Solomon was dead, Frank Morelli was reduced to a regional lieutenant, and Buccola was the most powerful mafioso in New England. Lombardo, who had escaped prosecution for the murders of Frank Wallace and his henchman, was trying his hand in the restaurant business in the North End while Buccola operated out of his home territory in the East End. Lombardo also headed most of the family's loan sharking operations as well as their illegal gambling for years before he stepped back from crime in the mid-1950s. In Providence, Morelli remained in a very powerful local position until he too retired in 1947, making Buccola even more powerful. Not much is known for certain about the New England Family in the 1940s, but that decade did see the rise of many mobsters who would end up becoming important figures in later years. One of these men was Joe Barboza, who would go on to cause major headaches for the family in the future. But of all the mafiosi who were out to make a name for themselves in these years, one Worcester-born member of the Providence faction rose above the rest. He had the mentoring of the respected don Iacone, won the position that Frank Morelli had vacated in Providence, and eventually was selected to run the entire New England operation. His name was Raymond L. S. Patriarca.

CHAPTER 2
THE RISE OF RAYMOND PATRIARCA

Raymond Patriarca is, without a doubt, the mafioso that we know the most about from the New England Family. Whereas his predecessors always carried an aura of mystery around them, making it difficult for historians to recover evidence about how they operated, Raymond Patriarca ended up becoming something of a celebrity in his lifetime. Notoriety and face recognition aren't the best qualities to possess when trying to run a criminal empire, but Patriarca nonetheless succeeded in taking the New England Mafia to all-new heights. He was so influential that the organization he ran ended up adopting his name—even today, the New England Mafia is known as the Patriarca Crime Family. Patriarca was certainly a successful man, and his reign coincided with a period that is generally regarded as a golden age for both the regional and national Mafia, but he and his contemporaries had to face new challenges that the bosses of the 1920s and 30s never did. Most notably, a coordinated and concerted effort by law enforcement to expose and destroy organized crime, which was an effort supported at the highest levels of government. Putting the names and faces of bosses all over the media was a part of this effort, and served to make Mafia leadership feel uneasy, paranoid, and exposed. So, before Patriarca's reign was over, he had become a public figure. He had always been a respected and recognizable member of his community in Providence, but the Patriarca name became tainted. However, before all this, Raymond was just a small-time gangster making a living in Worcester and Providence, and it didn't seem that he was destined to become boss. What does seem likely is that he was always destined to be a criminal.

"I Guess I Drifted a Little..."

In February of 1938, a robbery took place at a jewelry store in Brookline, Massachusetts, just west of Boston. It wasn't a typical nighttime robbery with discretion and a degree of finesse. It was flagrant, out in the open, and right in the middle of business hours. Well over $10,000 in cash, jewelry, and gold was stolen from the displays and store vault by two armed men. They forced the owner and employees of Wallbank Jewellers to cooperate under threat of death. One of these men holding the guns was 29-year-old Raymond Patriarca. With the considerable haul secured, the pair then decided to force the witnesses in the store to remove their clothes which they then also stole, likely to prevent them from exiting the store and witnessing their escape. To top things off, Patriarca and his co-conspirator tossed their loot into the back of the store owner's car and made off with that too. Just 11 months earlier, Raymond and his crew were involved in a payroll heist at Oxford Print. The men threatened the workers, stole yet another car to make their getaway, and this time they even took a hostage to make sure they gave up the payroll prints. If it wasn't already clear by the late 1930s, it was now: Raymond Patriarca loved stealing.

His relationship with theft went back a long time, dating back to at least his teenage years. But even he would admit later in life that something happened to him that may have helped make him the way he was. Born in Worcester, Massachusetts in 1908, Patriarca lived in a predominantly Italian ghetto that would have a considerable Mafia presence in later years. His surroundings were much the same when the family relocated to Atwells Avenue in Providence, Rhode Island. His father, Eleuterio, originally ran a liquor store and so became an active illegal liquor distributor during the early years of Prohibition, but he was not a big player in the city. He lived outside the law to provide for his family, but it did not necessarily doom young Raymond to a life of crime. Eleuterio's sons were already getting into trouble as teenagers, but their father was always there to help them and bail them out of jail when necessary. Then, in 1925, the senior Patriarca suddenly died, and Raymond was left without a father. According to Patriarca himself, this is when his life began to truly go off the rails: "I lost my father, and I guess I drifted a little…" (quoted in Songini, 2015).

It wasn't long after Eleuterio's death that Raymond devoted himself fully to the criminal lifestyle which he had only dabbled in in childhood. His crimes got bigger and what was once petty theft became armed robbery and grand theft auto. He even followed in his late father's footsteps and got involved in Prohibition-era bootlegging. Given his talents, it's unsurprising that Raymond spent most of his time hijacking transport trucks and stealing liquor shipments from other gangsters running booze through Rhode Island. In fact, Prohibition has the honor of being the first law that Raymond was put away for violating. It was just a year after his father's death, and he was slapped with just a one-month stay in a Connecticut jailhouse and a couple hundred dollars in fines. Evidently, it was not nearly enough to deter the young man, as he began his lifelong trend of violating his probation almost immediately after leaving jail and making his way back to

Providence. He earned a reputation around Providence as a notorious gambler and he also joined with his brother Joseph in several pimping ventures, all of which got him in trouble at some point. These run-ins with the law would plague him for decades to come.

At some point, Raymond linked up with the Providence-based Morelli brothers, Frank and Joe, and their gang. At the time, the Morellis were a relatively small-time group of disorganized thugs and heisters, but these were the years that Frank was working to bring the city's rackets under his control. With Patriarca's help, the gang began to take on the look of an actual *organized* crime Family. In later years, when Morelli began to step back from his active role in overseeing crime in Providence, it was to Raymond Patriarca that he chose to cede most of his lucrative enterprises to. Around the same time that Patriarca was associating with the Morellis, he also began working under the respected Worcester boss Frank Iacone, who mentored him in running a crew and crime empire. Raymond did plenty of bootlegging in those days and spent a lot of time running rum interstate from Rhode Island into Massachusetts on behalf of don Iacone. Aside from this, he also began making money on the side. In fact, he played both sides of the rum-running game: He both hijacked other gangs' liquor trucks and worked security for the liquor shipments of other gangs, including the Irish (although it's been reported that Raymond made himself available to those planning to ambush his shipments and, for a fee, he would allow the trucks to be stolen without a fight). He also did some pimping across state lines with his brother, which carried surprisingly little return considering the severity of interstate human trafficking. All of these things got him in trouble (for the transportation of women across state lines, both he and his brother earned a stay in a penitentiary in Atlanta) as he piled up an impressive rap sheet. Despite his recklessness, Raymond Patriarca was heading into the 1930s well-positioned for a meteoric rise through the criminal underworld.

Il Patrone, A Made Guy

With Iacone's tutelage, the time had come by 1929 to initiate Raymond Patriarca as an official member of the Mafia. When he was "made," it wasn't just a New England affair. By the 1930s, Raymond was already well-known in New York Mafia circles. This was before the days of the Commission, so it wasn't necessary for Patriarca's induction to be approved, but he nonetheless had the blessing of the New York leadership. The weight that Patriarca's name carried in New York only increased in later years, and although he had proven to be a somewhat careless and brash criminal at times, he had also earned a reputation as a calculated, diplomatic, and even-handed leader. This allowed him to be a trusted voice and confidant later in his career, and he even bragged at one point that he held sway over the Five Families and that few big decisions in the Big Apple weren't made without his approval. This may have been an exaggeration on his part, but it is certainly true that his opinion mattered to many high-ranking bosses.

Raymond Patriarca was now a made man, and as such, he was more powerful than ever. Considered untouchable (except by other made guys and, of course, law enforcement), he could operate in his home territory with much more confidence. If anyone crossed him, they would have the Providence faction to deal with, and later, it would be the entire New England Mafia. He had a sense of security, impunity, and power, and his taunting and menacing of law enforcement rose in kind—by the early 1930s, Raymond was already atop Providence's list of public enemies. He and his crew dabbled in just about everything from bootlegging (until 1933) to extorting illegal gambling clubs, but his guilty pleasure was always stealing. Sometimes it didn't even matter what he was stealing (as we've seen, he was not above lifting the literal shirt off a man's back). When Raymond staged the bold and successful daytime heist at the Wallbank Jewellers, it took him less than a week to plan and stage yet another robbery scheme, this time at United Optical, a company that produced luxury eyeglasses. He and his partner at least had the good sense to wait until nightfall to attempt the break-in, but the plan was doomed anyway. Loud noises convinced nearby residents to report suspicious activity and before Raymond could grab the goods and make a getaway (likely in yet another stolen car), a dispatch of officers entered the building. Raymond hid but was eventually discovered and arrested after trying to conceal his identity. As it turned out, Raymond was still a bit reckless: When the officers searched his vehicle, they found merchandise that would eventually be linked back to the jeweler in Brookline.

So, Raymond was off to jail again to await his fair trial. He wasn't there for long before he got someone to post his bail so he could at least be a free man until he faced the jury for his failed eyeglass heist. Almost immediately though, Raymond was implicated in the jewelry store robbery, which was confirmed personally by the owner of the establishment who immediately recognized Raymond's apparently unmasked face. Rhode Island police were given the order to arrest him once again, and luckily for them, Raymond was a reliably compulsive gambler who did a poor job controlling his habits. They found him quickly and easily, betting on the horses at a Rhode Island racetrack. Raymond was back in jail and when it came time to take the stand and defend himself for the crimes he had been convincingly accused of, he chose to plead guilty. The sentence he received carried a maximum penalty of five years in a prison cell. The punishment likely would've been much harsher had he chosen to fight the charges, which would've been a lengthy process. Besides, the indisputable incriminating evidence suggested that he didn't stand much of a chance in court anyway. Raymond was off to Charlestown State Prison in Boston.

Neither Raymond nor the Family were keen to have him behind bars for the long haul. Joe Patriarca—Raymond's brother and frequent criminal accomplice—together with the New England mob enlisted the help of a Boston lawyer, Dan Coakley. Coakley had less than a stellar reputation in the legal community, especially among Massachusetts' state prosecutors, but there's no doubt that he had a talent for making the problems of criminals disappear, so long as they had the cash and were willing to bend the rules. It was decided that even though Raymond had essentially admitted to the charges, his legal team would pursue a pardon. Amazingly, Coakley actually pulled it off. With some faked letters and a bit of underhanded legal chicanery, Raymond was released from prison just a few days before the end of 1938, well before he served even a fifth of his sentence.

Raymond wasn't completely out of the woods in 1939. There were still serious questions regarding his involvement in past crimes, particularly his affinity for stealing cars (it was something he did both on its own and during the course of other crimes). Authorities in Massachusetts were, unsurprisingly, not happy with the result of Raymond's previous conviction and were out to nab him on anything that would put him back in a jail cell. Outwardly though, Raymond was trying to go straight. The saga of his multiple arrests, guilty plea, and ultimate release had become headline news by this point, and the media in New England was eager to hear his input on the situation. He told them his sole focus was making amends and settling down for a quiet life, the latter of which he actually did when he married Helen Mancini (her last name is sometimes spelled "Mandella"). As for his going straight, he at least wasn't in New England long enough afterward to cause much more trouble. After the wedding ceremony, he and his new wife took off for Miami for an extended honeymoon while Rhode Island and Massachusetts police were still investigating him. Unfortunately for him, his notoriety stretched past New England and police in southern Florida would be keeping a close watch on the newlyweds.

It should have been easy for Raymond to at least avoid arrest while he was in Miami—so long as he did nothing wrong, there would be no reason to apprehend him unless authorities in New England indicted him again and issued an extradition request. Yet for some unknown reason, when he was stopped and questioned about his business in Miami and where he lived, he offered them a fake home address. Already suspicious of Patriarca, it didn't take much digging to find the empty parking lot where the mafioso had claimed his house should be. It was a bizarre thing for him to do while being actively surveilled but in any case, it was enough for the police to pick him up on suspicion.

While in custody, Florida authorities got in touch with their counterparts in New England, and it was determined that Raymond should be sent back to Massachusetts to face trial once again. Police there had a fresh indictment for grand theft auto waiting for him when he arrived back in the state with his Boston police chaperone (his new bride was still back in Miami, stranded and probably very confused). Also waiting for him was a parade of media paparazzi trying to get photos and sound bites of the notorious criminal who, as the papers correctly suggested, may have received a pardon under false pretenses. The issue with his pardon was becoming a serious concern—if forgeries were discovered in the documents, it could endanger the careers of several New England politicians and other officials who had been in the Mafia's pocket.

The media attention that followed Raymond's forced arrival back in New England caused a cascading effect on his legal woes. His name and face constantly being in the papers led to more folks recognizing him, which led to him being implicated in even more past crimes. Raymond would spend the rest of 1939 as well as the early 1940s trying desperately to evade charges and clear his name, but it was no use. He was going to face serious charges, and among them was attempted murder. This charge was likely the result of his constantly threatening those he was robbing with death if they didn't cooperate. He was constantly being released and rearrested and whenever one of the cases against him fell apart, it seemed another charge was always there to take its place. Ultimately, Raymond went to trial for two cases of robbery which he once again pleaded guilty to. Near the end of 1941, Raymond was off to prison once again and this time there would be no phony letters from community priests testifying to his character, nor would there be any ill-gotten pardons to get him out early. He served his time and was finally released into the public in May of 1944.

Raymond was a free man (at least for now) and had a lot of work to do. As it turned out, he got busy building up both his own family and his Mafia Family—just a year after his release, the woman that Raymond unwillingly abandoned in Miami about six years prior gave birth to his son, Raymond Patriarca Jr., who was commonly known simply as "Junior." Junior would also have a significant role to play in the fate of the New England Mafia, and in later years he would be the one to inherit his father's criminal empire. But before that could happen, Raymond Sr. needed to build such an empire. Another testament to the misguided nature of the American justice system of the early decades of the 20th century, exactly no one was convinced that Raymond's stay in prison would reform him or correct the wayward path he had been on since at least the early 1920s. Indeed, upon his release he was more ambitious in his criminal activity than ever before and sought to regain control of his former rackets that had been divided up amongst the Family since his conviction. It was at this point that Raymond began collecting his close-knit group of associates who would later form the bulk of the leadership when the Patriarca name was on top. Among these men were Louis Taglianetti and Henry (originally Enrico) Tameleo, a made guy who was tied to the Bonannos in New York but was active in Massachusetts, Rhode Island, and likely Connecticut as well. Tameleo had earned himself the nickname "Referee," or "The Ref," for being a conciliatory voice between the New England and New York Families.

Together, these three men—along with their crews—began to bulk out the Providence faction, at this point still controlled by the aging Frank Morelli and his brothers. By the time Raymond was out of prison in '44, it was clear that the Morelli era in Providence was near its close, as its leadership became reckless and was plagued with infighting. Luckily, in his effort to establish connections and support across the regions, Raymond had ingratiated himself with Phil Buccola, the boss of the combined Boston-Providence operations. So, when it became obvious in 1947 that it was time for Morelli to step aside, it was Raymond Patriarca that Buccola favored to fill his spot and become the next Providence underboss. Raymond now had the favor of Worcester wiseguy Frank Iacone and the boss in Boston, but the connections he made in these years went beyond New England: He had also associated himself with Frank Costello, head of the organization that later became the Genovese Family. With huge support both within Rhode Island and out of state, Providence was Patriarca's for the taking.

Aside from Raymond's campaign to reorganize the Providence faction under him, Mafia activity had been steady, quiet, and profitable for years. The beginning of the 1950s, however, marked a new age for the Mafia. It was the beginning of the era of celebrity prosecutors and public figures trying to make a name for themselves through high-profile, often televised, investigations and trials. This phenomenon continued for decades and was perhaps the most destructive development for the American Mafia. In the 1980s, lawyers such as Rudolph Giuliani leveraged their success in prosecuting mob bosses to transition into successful political careers. For instance, Giuliani used his success in taking down New York City's Five Families as a launching pad to become the city's mayor. In Patriarca's era though, it was the Kefauver Committee hearings of 1950 that first sounded the alarm. Estes Kefauver, a relatively unknown senator out of Tennessee, introduced a resolution that proposed the formation of a senate committee with a mandate to investigate Mafia-related interstate crime. His proposal very nearly fell apart before it saw the light of day, but after some maneuvering and a razor-thin senate vote, the Kefauver Committee was created. Its members were mostly lawyers by trade and included senators Alex Wiley, Lester Hunt, Charles Tobey, Herb O'Conor, Rudolph Halley as Chief Counselor, and Kefauver himself.

Beginning in New York, the committee started calling in alleged Mafia bosses to testify before the Senate. The hearings were televised and highly publicized, which put even the most stone-faced mafiosi under a crushing amount of pressure; the likes of which they had never experienced. Plenty had been to court, but none had ever had to defend themselves while, for all they knew, the entire nation was watching and reporters captured their every move. Unfortunately for Raymond, his closest ally in NYC—Frank Costello—was the most tripped up by the affair. The successor of the legend Lucky Luciano made a fool of himself as cameras caught him fidgeting, sweating, repeatedly contradicting himself, and generally coming off as extremely suspicious. In 1950, no one from within the Mafia had yet admitted publicly to its existence—La Cosa Nostra still had an aura of mystery surrounding it, but this embarrassment gave the entire nation a hint that the Mafia was indeed real, and that the stories they had been hearing for decades were true. Costello's reputation never recovered after his testimony and as a result, the Patriarca influence in New York was weakened. But Raymond had much bigger problems on the horizon. After the hearings were wrapped up in New York City, it was announced that Kefauver, his committee, and the myriad film crews were packing up and heading for New England.

This news was troublesome to everyone in Massachusetts and Rhode Island with an empire to lose. This was particularly true for those who had been mentioned by name, which included the elders Buccola and Iacone, plus Raymond himself. Buccola, being at his advanced age and being the man in charge of the entire regional operation, was particularly stressed. He knew that he wouldn't be able to continue in his position for much longer without health complications interfering. Besides, it would have been in his best interest to vacate the top spot to let the heat die down. Buccola seems to have favored Patriarca, his underboss in Providence, as his heir. Raymond was one of the few gangsters in Rhode Island who held sway and commanded respect. Given his reputation in Massachusetts and New York, it was logical to choose him. Sometime in 1952, prominent veterans of La Cosa Nostra met to discuss the affair, and ultimately they decided to accept Buccola's nomination of the big man in Providence as successor to the New England Mafia. The decision was met with much fanfare as Iacone arranged a large celebration in Raymond's honor which attracted big underworld names from New York, Philadelphia, Chicago, and elsewhere. By 1954 when Buccola fully retired and went back to his native Sicily, Raymond Patriarca was the boss of his own Mafia Family, one which would eventually carry his name.

CHAPTER 3
THE PATRIARCA CRIME FAMILY

After the celebrations were over and bosses from all over the eastern states had paid their respects to New England's newest don, Patriarca began the most significant reorganization of the region's criminal underground since the creation of the Commission and the merging of the Boston and Providence factions. It was a new era for the Family, one which brought plenty of new fortunes but also fresh, potentially fatal challenges. Patriarca was an effective leader and he operated a relatively smooth business, but certain aspects were outside of his control. After surviving the publicity nightmare caused by the 1950 Senate testimonies, things would only get worse for organized crime in America. A new generation of crusaders rose to confront and expose the Mafia that had been shrouded in unanswered questions for years. Police and federal agents began using aggressive tactics and tools to nab their guys, and frankly, they terrified the Family bosses. By the mid-1960s, Mafia life had changed permanently. Before Raymond was even out of the game, the empire he created was already beginning to crack under the pressure that had been building since Frank Costello first stammered his way through his self-defense against Estes Kefauver and his personal Justice League.

The New Providence Regime

When Raymond fully inherited Buccola's empire in 1954, he was already beginning to tire of the demands of Mafia life. Now that he was boss, this pressure was felt even more acutely. He would now personally face more scrutiny from law enforcement than ever before and now, he had much more to lose. Raymond was already quite reserved and generally wary of people he didn't know, but now he was forced to trust even fewer people—one new tactic of the government was the relentless pursuit of potential informants or disgruntled mafiosi willing to flip and become state witnesses. As a result, the new regime in Providence was defined by an utmost commitment to secrecy and discretion. Raymond kept his inner circle incredibly tight, and those outside of Providence were often on the outside looking in. He also moved the New England Family's "headquarters" away from Boston to his home city. Although the criminal marketplace was considerably bigger in Boston, Providence was where Raymond felt the most comfortable and secure, qualities that seemed more valuable than ever in those days. This was a drastic change: The Family's seat of power would remain in the Rhode Island capital city for decades.

Raymond operated a bit differently from other bosses. He proved to be adept at keeping his top guys and their underlings strictly in line, despite the incredibly wide distribution of the Family operations across several New England states. Further, his general trust issues led him to completely disregard the long-standing Mafia tradition of working exclusively with Italians (in some more strict cases, even Italian heritage wasn't enough—one needed to be full-blooded Sicilian on both sides). The Patriarca Crime Family, as it came to be called, was known to work and associate with anyone, regardless of their ethnicity, so long as they were deemed reliable and could be trusted by Raymond. Honor and character were paramount, and employing those with loose lips or questionable integrity was out of the question. Unfortunately, as we'll see, more than a few rats slipped through Raymond's vetting attempts. For now though, business had to go on and Raymond was tasked with guiding his Family through a new decade and a new era.

Fearing the potential downfall of his ally Costello in New York City, Patriarca soon began building new relationships to avoid being isolated from the Families out west. He formed close ties with the Profaci (soon to be renamed Colombo) Family which gave Patriarca a valuable support base in the event anyone challenged his new position. In the interest of closing the ranks, he began filling his subordinate leadership positions with the crew he had first begun to assemble when he was released from prison in the 1940s. Tameleo was made underboss of operations in Providence, and it seems that Anthony Santaniello was given charge of the now-subsidiary Boston faction. The promotion of Tameleo with his close ties to the Bonannos also helped garner support in the Empire State. After Vito Genovese predictably overthrew Costello (he willingly stepped down after Genovese orchestrated a failed hit on him), Patriarca still maintained a working business relationship with the Family.

With the Providence-NYC connection secure, Raymond had his own Family affairs to tend to. For the most part, the Patriarcas continued to be active in all the typical Mafia rackets, which included gambling, loansharking, labor unions (eventually), prostitution, and even the production of pornography. The days of bootlegging alcohol were long dead, but Patriarca men eventually found new addictive substances to peddle. According to the mafioso-turned-witness Vincent Teresa, Patriarca had warned all of his men to stay away from the narcotics trade but just like with liquor prohibition, the potential profit to be made off of drug prohibition was too tempting to resist. If it is true that Patriarca was vehemently against drug dealing, it was a wise move—when the 1980s hit, their involvement in the narcotics industry became one of the main reasons for the Mafia's eventual collapse.

Part of the transformation of the New England Family into the Patriarca Family was the creation of several new, large front businesses. Raymond had to try to rehabilitate his image as an upstanding, honest businessman and at the same time needed to launder all the illicit profit that he was keen to take in. The two largest of these fronts were two sides of the same coin: The National Cigarette Service, which obviously distributed cigarettes, and the Coin-O-Matic Distributing Co., which installed coin-operated machines in businesses. These included pinballs and arcade-style machines, as well as vending machines which, of course, dispensed his cigarettes. These companies alone were profitable and the Family used classic Mafia extortion tactics to ensure that it was Raymond's cigarettes that people were buying and that it was Raymond's machines that sold them. Coin-O-Matic formed the backbone of Raymond's "legitimate" business empire and, tending to live modestly and avoid excess, he conducted the vast majority of the Family business out of his small Coin-O-Matic office room. This room became almost like folklore: Eventually it, and the entire Patriarca Family, would be referred to simply as "The Office." Aside from these businesses, the Family's other fronts included a dump, some nightclubs, and a textile plant.

As part of his effort to create a favorable image of himself, Raymond kept up a decent public persona throughout the 1950s. He was philanthropic and was often involved in high-profile charity work (at least when business fortune allowed). The facade of an upstanding and respectable man that Raymond wore was successful, and over time he came to be seen as a leader in his community. His reputation for being a skilled arbitrator already made him a trusted presence in disagreements between other gangsters and mafiosi, but folks would often turn to Raymond to settle even non-Mafia disputes in Providence. Henry Tameleo, the Patriarca underboss, seems to have functioned as a sort of diplomat or envoy for Raymond personally. According to Barboza, the enforcer and hitman-turned-witness, Tameleo was the one who ensured that the public image of both Raymond and his associates remained admirable and impeccable. He was also tasked with making sure Patriarca underlings remained happy with leadership, toed the line, and did not turn rebellious.

For years after Raymond took over, this strategy and regimen were very successful. As a result, his power grew considerably in these years and Providence was no longer a backwater of the Mafia world. Where the New England Mafia was once small and disorganized, it was now powerful, centralized around Rhode Island, and earned the respect of the Five Families in New York. The clearest sign of this is that, even in the wake of Buccola's retirement, Patriarca was able to keep the other powerful New York and New Jersey Families from encroaching on his territory. Most importantly, he accomplished this through diplomacy rather than violence. What could have evolved into an interstate turf war was settled with an agreement that the bosses respected for decades. Using the Connecticut River as a dividing line, the eastern portion was the domain of the Patriarcas, and everything to the west was free game for the other friendly Families. Some Families were able to operate across the river as well, so long as they had the blessing of Il Patrone. The

Genoveses, for example, directly controlled Springfield, MA, as well as regions of Connecticut, including the city of Hartford.

The overlaps ran even deeper: In Worcester (one of the main Patriarca Family cities and a place that Raymond used to frequent) it was Carlo Mastrototaro who was selected to take over for the elderly Frank Iacone. It turns out that Iacone had joined Frank Costello in the club of victims of the Kefauver Committee. When the panel of senators held their planned hearing for the Worcester don, something about his testimony left them unsatisfied and suspicious. Under the direction of Chairman Kefauver, the Internal Revenue Service launched an investigation into Iacone's tax returns and came up with enough to indict him for evasion—they reportedly found a discrepancy of hundreds of thousands of dollars worth of unpaid income tax. In early 1953 he was facing charges to which he pleaded guilty. Iacone, who had been active since the Prohibition days and had long dominated much of Massachusetts' illegal gambling, was gone and his position vacated.

This was definitely a blow to the Family, as Iacone brought to the table huge profits, reliable counsel, and more than a few important connections he had built over the decades. Especially within Worcester, he was nearly untouchable by local law enforcement. Most notably, Worcester police Lieutenant Bill Massei had formed a close personal and business relationship with Iacone. Incredibly, since 1940 Massei was the appointed head of the crime unit specifically meant to tackle the city's organized gambling rackets, which were run by Iacone. As a result, he was for years able to operate with near impunity, all the while the man who was supposed to be investigating him assured the city's residents that illegal gambling in Worcester was a myth. Indeed, Iacone was a difficult man to replace; and not only because of the people he had in his pocket. Ultimately though, Worcester native Mastrototaro filled the void. Mastrototaro was a seasoned, decorated veteran of the Second World War (he had been a Marine since 1939 when the war began) and was also a long-serving captain in the Genovese Family. With Raymond's approval, Mastrototaro replaced his former mentor and apparently performed admirably, holding the position for decades. In this role, the new Worcester don served the interests of both the Patriarcas in Providence and the Genoveses in New York.

Clearly, Raymond knew how to make peace and, despite his notorious temper, he could be very tactful. But when all else failed, the Patriarcas relied on intimidation and violence just like every other Family. When they needed intimidation and muscle, they turned to their enforcers. The most prominent of these were John Nazarian and Joe Barboza. Nazarian was known to be crazy, which earned him the nickname "Mad Dog." This usually meant that the threat of Nazarian coming after you was more than enough to make sure you paid what was owed to the Family. On the surface, it appeared as if Raymond's "legitimate" businesses were the sources of the Family's wealth, but behind the scenes it was Mad Dog Nazarian and his ragtag crew of questionably loyal thugs who ensured they saw steady flows of profit. Because Nazarian's name was known across the eastern states as belonging to an erratic criminal who killed for cheap and didn't care about witnesses, Raymond had the difficult task of keeping him at arm's length to avoid being implicated in his wild exploits, yet still close enough to control him and ensure his violent tendencies were directed in the best interests of the Family.

Joe Barboza was no less frightening than Nazarian. A son of Portuguese immigrants, Barboza was never a made man in the

Family (nor was Nazarian for that matter), but he did end up having a significant impact on its future. He was quite a bit younger than Nazarian, but his affinity for delivering savage beatings (and the account in which he reportedly bit the ear of a man after being told by Tameleo to keep his hands off him) had also earned him an unfriendly nickname. He was "The Animal," and he was a reliable hitman for hire to all manner of New England criminals in the late 1950s and 1960s. He was an imposing figure too, with a large frame that he used during his stint as a pro boxer. This made him a valuable extortionist and, like Nazarian, his reputation often got the work done for him. In fact, Barboza's criminal history was even more sensational than Nazarian's in some ways. He had been breaking the law since before he was a teenager and his first prison sentence came before he was even legal drinking age. But before his sentence—which was handed down to him at 18 years old—was concluded, he had formed a crew of several other inmates and together they staged a daring escape. They broke out of their cells, assaulted and beat the guards, and slipped out into the streets of Boston before they were all rounded up again. By 1958, he had linked up with the Patriarcas and Stephen Flemmi, a member of the notorious Irish Winter Hill Gang. Winter Hill was founded in the mid-1950s by Buddy McLean and was ruled between 1966 and 1979 by the infamous Irish-Italian gangster Howard Winter.

With these two brutes in his arsenal, and with his most trusted guys running operations in Providence, Boston, and Worcester, things were looking solid for Raymond Patriarca and his Family as they entered the 1960s. The income from their diverse array of rackets enabled them to expand their influence across multiple states. They gained ground in their home states of Rhode Island and Massachusetts, as well as in peripheral territories such as

Connecticut. Later, they extended their reach to Maine and New Hampshire, where Orlando Napolitano's Portland Family became affiliated with the far larger and more powerful Patriarcas. Despite the Kefauver hearings causing a stir in the underworld from Los Angeles to Providence, things carried on in a relatively familiar fashion for years (although Raymond was a bit more paranoid) and the New England Mafia prospered under steady, even-handed guidance. But this peace too came to an end, and things quickly threatened to spiral out of control. The coming years would see Raymond, as well as plenty of other top Mafia guys, become terrified of law enforcement and their new tools and techniques, including witness hunting, wiretaps, and electronic surveillance devices. It was yet another new era, one where some bosses went mad from the constant fear that they were being monitored by someone or something. Much of this can be traced back to events in New York City, particularly the infamous and ill-fated Apalachin Meeting of 1957.

The Witness You Can't Kill

On the 25th of October in 1957, Albert Anastasia was shot dead in his chair by two men as he awaited a haircut at a Manhattan barbershop. Anastasia was one of the most veteran figures in the American Mafia and in New York, he was considered royalty of the old school. He was head of the powerful organization that would soon be known as the Gambino Family, and he was the most powerful gangster in New York's waterfront districts. Unfortunately for him, the power he had accumulated over the years stood little chance when confronted with the ambition of the younger generation. Vito Genovese, apparently unsatisfied with the failed hit on Frank Costello months earlier, banded together with

Carlo Gambino to carry out the assassination of Anastasia. With the seasoned veteran out of the picture, it was Gambino who took over the remnants of his former empire. But as it turned out, the hit was also part of a grander scheme, orchestrated by Genovese, to become New York City's premiere Mafia boss.

With Anastasia out of the picture, the question of what to do with the rackets he controlled and the people from whom Anastasia was still owed money was a troubling hurdle to overcome. His empire was vast, and the solution wasn't as simple as appointing a new head of the Family, though Gambino probably would have preferred that to be the case. Further, developments in the government's assault on Mafia activities had gone unaddressed for too long. For these reasons, Vito Genovese called a meeting of Family heads from across the nation, as well as their top made men. The purpose was ostensibly to discuss these issues which were pertinent to the functioning of the Mafia across the states (as well as in Montreal, Canada—the home of the Rizzuto Family), but it's generally agreed that this was part of a major power play by Genovese to solidify himself as the de facto *capo di tutti capi* of the underworld. Genovese was a new boss in New York and had to replace the widely-respected Costello, so organizing and calling this meeting was meant as a signal to bosses across the nation that he was capable of calling the shots and arbitrating on vital matters. So it was that in November of 1957, the nation's foremost made men from New York, New Jersey, California, Ohio, Florida, Illinois, Pennsylvania, Kansas, and elsewhere convened at one of the biggest criminal meet-ups in American history.

The meeting was held at the home of Joseph Barbara, known by his friends as Joe the Barber. He was another mobster of the old school and was originally of the Castellammarese faction decades ago, so his hosting was a natural choice. It wasn't Joe's only home—he was the boss of the Bufalino Family based out of the Scranton Wilkes-Barre area of Pennsylvania, but he always maintained a presence in NYC. His Empire State home was in the Apalachin neighborhood in New York's Tioga County. As a result, the summit would go down in history as the "Apalachin Meeting." Unfortunately, it didn't go down in history as a resounding success, but rather as one of the biggest blunders in organized crime. Before everything was said and done, dozens of mafiosi and bosses from across the country were detained by New York police and some 20 of them were charged, convicted, and fined. What was originally meant to be Genovese's grand gesture of domination had become a farce, and both his and Barbara's reputations took a hit. It also seriously damaged the credibility of the decades-old claim that the Mafia was imaginary and that organized crime was a non-issue—reportedly, there were over 100 of the nation's most wanted criminals at Barbara's estate that day.

There are many theories that have been formed in the years since Apalachin that contend that the entire calamity was a setup, likely by another mafioso. This would make sense given that there were likely more than a few rival mobsters who would've liked to see Vito Genovese's ego cut down to size, but such a move would have jeopardized the operation of the entire Mafia, everywhere. And, since so many bosses were known to be in attendance, the destruction of the leadership of nearly every major Family could've been achieved in one fell swoop. It was also assumed for a long time that local police simply happened upon the meeting after noticing the strange number of fancy, out-of-state luxury vehicles parked at the vast property. As it turns out though, New York state troopers had already been keeping an eye on the Barbara estate for quite some time. After a high-ranking member of the Bonanno Family was recorded visiting and leaving Barbara's home, law enforcement made it a habit to include the estate in their routine patrols. Further, a state trooper by the name of Edgar Croswell had been pursuing leads on Barbara, and prior to the meeting's scheduled date he had discovered a suspicious number of room reservations made at hotels across the city, all under the name of Barbara's son. He relayed this information to his superiors who realized immediately that something big was about to happen.

When patrolmen reported the strange fleet of vehicles at the estate, it was time to move. Officers began preemptively running the plate numbers of the vehicles which, before long, revealed that more than a few of them belonged to either wanted criminals or criminal suspects. This was all the pretext that was needed, and so a roadblock was set up and officers prepared to forcefully enter Barbara's estate. All the while, inside the house Vito Genovese was unwittingly making his long-awaited grandstand in the presence of the nation's premiere criminals. Unfortunately for the New England Family, Raymond Patriarca and his consigliere Frank Cucchiara (the same Cucchiara that Messina had partnered with years earlier) were among those criminals in attendance. Police attempted to arrest everyone in attendance, but that didn't stop dozens of them from attempting to escape. Some shuffled past officers to their vehicles only to drive directly into a roadblock. Some of the more frantic and desperate decided to make a getaway on foot, attempting to sprint through the fields behind Barbara's manor. Dozens of the most feared men in America, clad in expensive shoes and designer clothes, were reduced to dodging cops like petty street thugs. It's not clear exactly what happened to Raymond at the meeting, or how and if he attempted an escape, but he was identified as an attendee and if he was apprehended, he was soon a free man.

Despite years of fighting unfavorable media coverage and (correct) accusations of malfeasance, this was the most exposed Raymond, and the Mafia, had ever been. The entire underworld was shaken and the Patriarcas now feared more severe legal action. With Raymond's criminal history, it would be a difficult task convincing anyone that his presence at a meeting of known gangsters was pure happenstance. Perhaps the biggest knock-on effect of the Apalachin Meeting, though, was the fact that Director of the FBI J. Edgar Hoover was now *forced* to take the threat of the Mafia presence in America seriously. This was largely due to the insistence of Robert F. Kennedy, future Attorney General and brother of future U.S. President John F. Kennedy. For years, Hoover had repeatedly and publicly denied the possibility that an extensive criminal network like the Mafia could exist in the United States. There are a couple of potential reasons for this. Many assumed that the Mafia's growth during Director Hoover's tenure at the Federal Bureau was a source of shame for him. If this is true, it would have been easier to simply deny their existence rather than admit that they were there and he was powerless to stop them. More likely, though, is that Hoover denied their existence because he himself had gathered more than a few Mafia connections as a result of his alleged degenerate gambling habits and affinity for prostitutes. Whatever the case may be, his hand was forced after Apalachin. Neither he nor mafiosi themselves could credibly claim that La Cosa Nostra was nothing more than a legend from the old country.

The aforementioned era of anti-Mafia crusaders was definitely in full swing. The year after the abortive Apalachin Meeting, the U.S. Senate called Raymond Patriarca to testify before the McClellan

Committee on labor crime. It was a select committee that was formed in early 1957, meant to investigate organized crime and American labor unions. The committee took the name of John McClellan, a Democratic senator out of Arkansas who had been investigating the Teamsters; one of the nation's largest labor unions. Its goal had broadened since its formation and in February of 1958, the committee had their eyes on Patriarca. The answers he presented to the panel were less than satisfying—when asked how he acquired enough money, without taking loans, to start his various business enterprises, he credited his mother who apparently left him tens of thousands of dollars in cash as an unofficial inheritance. When asked why he chose a life of petty crime and robbery in his earlier years when he had so much money waiting for him, he once again blamed the tragedy of his father's death. Finally, when questioned about the well-known extortion tactics that Patriarca's underlings used to funnel revenue into his National Cigarette Service corporation, he simply pleaded ignorance. The chairmen, particularly Robert Kennedy, were incensed. Later, Raymond received a subpoena from another Senate committee.

The increased scrutiny on Patriarca in particular in years following his senate testimonies likely wasn't a coincidence. Around this time, probably in 1960, Raymond was allegedly chosen by national bosses to serve on the Mafia Commission. At the time, the government had an idea that the Commission existed but it was still a nebulous concept. Unfortunately, the combined stress of his senate subpoenas and his appointment to the Commission seems to have taken its toll on him in 1960 when he suffered cardiac arrest and was hospitalized. He remained in bad health for a while and to make matters worse, his underboss in Boston, Santaniello, died that same year. Now with two senior members out of the picture, the Family was in crisis. Needing a strong influence to keep order in Boston, it was Gennaro "Jerry" Angiulo who rose to fill Santaniello's spot. Jerry, the most prominent of his troupe of criminal siblings, was a Boston native and big-shot nightclub owner in the city. He was also a restaurateur, and his most popular place was a bar and grill called Jay's Lounge on Tremont Street in Boston. Because it was such a well-known Mafia hangout, it later became the target of extensive FBI wiretaps. Angiulo had steadily risen through the ranks of the Boston faction since the end of WWII and, even though he was not part of Raymond's insulated inner circle of counselors, he did eventually become the Family's underboss.

Unfortunately, Santaniello's death wasn't the only problem for Raymond in Boston. Unbeknownst to him, one of his guys there, Vincent Teresa, had become a police informant. Teresa, whose Mafia lineage went all the way back at least to his grandfather in Sicily, was well-connected and worked his way up to becoming a trusted enforcer in Henry/Enrico Tameleo's crew. He was a long-time criminal whose history of burglaries dates back to his grade school days. Though he did enlist in the Navy during WWII, he only did so at the tail end in 1945, and even then he was dishonorably discharged within 3 years. Needless to say, he was a bad egg. He managed to top out working as a kind of debt collector for Tameleo in Boston and Worcester, but this gig never seemed to be enough for him. He was definitely the right guy for the job, as few knew more about debt than Vincent Teresa: He was a full-blown, lifelong gambling addict since before he was kicked out of school in the 9th grade. He spent his free time racking up endless debt from various hustlers across Boston's North End and elsewhere, and when the money he earned collecting from other debtors wasn't enough to pay them back, he stole; which meant that he stole a lot. Unsurprisingly, this made him plenty of enemies in Massachusetts. But all of it couldn't feed his habit successfully—he was perpetually teetering on bankruptcy and he simply couldn't steal enough to keep him afloat.

All of this meant that Teresa was a perfect target for the FBI's witness hunt. Hoover had been begrudgingly directing his Bureau's agents to aggressively pursue any leads on made men or associates who might be willing to flip and inform on their bosses. Teresa, who plenty of people wanted dead and who was buried to his neck in debt, needed little convincing to begin feeding (often fabricated) information to his federal handlers. Promised a place in federal witness protection after his tenure was over, he also had less to fear from ballooning his list of enemies. By the first few years of the 1960s, Vincent Teresa had become a full-fledged Mafia rat. The campaign to flip inside guys accelerated after the election of John F. Kennedy to the White House in 1961. He quickly made his brother, Bobby Kennedy, the Attorney General and with this new executive and judicial power, Bobby set to work recruiting as many made guys as possible from across the Mafia hubs and building cases off of the information he received. When it came time to prosecute, the state would have a robust arsenal of first-hand witnesses willing to expose their peers to save themselves. Again, greed proved to be one of the Mafia's most self-destructive characteristics. The effects of this witness hunting process were felt most acutely in New York state, but Boston and Providence were clearly not spared.

In 1963, Teresa ratted out both Henry Tameleo and Jerry Angiulo to the FBI in exchange for a cash payment. Apparently, the two high-ranking Patriarca members were involved in a cartoonish scheme to heist valuable ivory and Chinese Ming dynasty-era jade. The reported value of the stolen goods ranged from about $50,000 to well over a million, but it was a significant amount regardless. Teresa was questioned in the investigation, during which he told police exactly where they could find the loot and was willing to implicate his own boss and the top guy in Boston. Vincent appears to have told the truth about this, at least: Both Tameleo and Angiulo's fingerprints were successfully lifted off the car in which they found the jade and ivory stashed, presumably as the pair waited for a suitable buyer. The police seized the goods, which of course caused problems in the Family as no one understood how the Feds could have known where it was.

Raymond ended up summoning both Tameleo and Angiulo to his Providence office to explain themselves and the debacle. The pair offered up excuses and theories, and it was suggested that perhaps someone ratted, but ultimately the two turned on each other under Raymond's disapproving gaze. Angiulo accused Tameleo of being reckless, and vice versa. It led to suspicions between Family members that would last for years and began a period of distrust between even the closest of associates. The Patriarca don, however, came to his own conclusion: The Feds must have discovered the location of the stolen goods by eavesdropping on his underlings via electronic surveillance devices. Raymond was already a paranoid man, but it seems that it went into overdrive after the jade bust. The New England boss told all his guys to be vigilant and utterly discrete in their dealings, and he closed off his inner circle even further. Frankly, he was terrified of wiretaps and hidden video recording devices, which he likened to witnesses that couldn't be killed, intimidated, or bribed. They were, in his eyes, a mafioso's kryptonite.

Angiulo was also succumbing to paranoia around this time, and was apparently frantic about the possibility of an IRS indictment. When he crunched his own numbers, he realized he could easily be found liable for over two years worth of tax fraud. With all of the media attention and high-profile, nationally televised senate hearings, all it would take is one tax agent to take an interest in the Angiulo name and his entire Boston operation could be in jeopardy. Then, also in 1963, an article published in the *Saturday Evening Post* dropped the jaws of just about every gangster from Providence to Boston. In uncomfortable detail, it described the illicit operations of Raymond Patriarca's empire and the myriad rackets they controlled for all their subscribers to read. Raymond's public image took yet another beating along with those of his top underlings. Even their "legitimate" rackets, especially National Cigarette, began to bleed profit because Raymond's name being attached to them scared business away (plus, with the strong-arm tactics of Nazarian directly exposed by the McClellan Committee, intimidation as a method of securing customers became less effective). Aside from the fronts, Raymond and Angiulo also personally lost a lot on some joint ventures, including some golf courses and a large investment in Vegas.

Financial woes continued for most of the top brass in New England, but the worst of 1963 was still to come. In October of that year, the efforts of Hoover and RFK paid dividends as the McClellan Committee gave way to the McClellan Hearings. These crusaders had long been searching for someone, a made man with enough credit (and dirt on them) who was willing to spill everything they knew about La Cosa Nostra. They eventually found their man in Joe Valachi, a soldier in the Genovese Family. Valachi was willing to tell all (even some fabricated bits) and his testimony was so consequential that the entire hearing process came to be known as the Valachi Hearings. During the hearings, Valachi became the first man in organized crime history to admit to the world, from the inside, that the Mafia existed. He went into great, frustrating detail about how the Mafia operated and how it was structured. He even detailed the most sacred of Mafia rituals which they performed at initiation ceremonies for new members. He spoke mostly about the Five Families, but in his testimony he also pointed to Raymond Patriarca by name as the top gangster of all the northeastern states.

Afterwards, Walter Stone—an official of the Rhode Island police—publicly poured salt in the wound by describing Patriarca as dangerous, underhanded, and absolutely not to be trusted. Angiulo got it bad in Boston too, where commissioner Ed McNamara publicly dropped Jerry's name when describing the illegal operations he was investigating. Jerry also had to fear for his safety after a botched attempt on his life at his home. The incident caused even more infighting in the Family, as Jerry began pointing fingers at other Patriarca members, specifically a made guy named Iacone. Some accounts claim that the veteran Frank Iacone was the one Jerry accused of the hit, but this is impossible since estate records detail Iacone's death in 1956. The name could have been a coincidence, but it's more likely he was a relative of Frank since, during an earlier encounter, Raymond clearly showed favor to him. During a meeting between this Iacone and Angiulo, Angiulo had supposedly severely insulted the other. When Iacone told Raymond about the run-in, he gave him explicit permission to murder Angiulo (Raymond's top man in Boston) on the spot if he ever spoke to him in that manner again. Raymond of course had to mediate the dispute, but his hasty and violent suggestion to Iacone was a sign of times to come—Raymond was losing his ability to arbitrate peacefully between his men.

Angiulo, still deeply troubled by the law and his various enemies, even considered fleeing the country to get away from it all, believing that "this thing of ours" would be easier back in Sicily with the old Families or up in Canada with the Cotronis and Rizzutos. The enforcer and Family associate Joe Barboza, too, was growing increasingly paranoid; both of being identified by police and of being murdered in the street. He allegedly went so far as to disguise himself in public for fear of someone recognizing him, often comically dressing up as an old lady. These fears wore him down over the years and eventually, like Vincent Teresa, he flipped. By 1967, Barboza was informing the FBI on the Patriarcas. As the story goes, Barboza was picked up on a weapons charge sometime after being released from jail in 1964. The Patriarcas didn't seem to mind, as they had seemingly grown tired of Barboza's shenanigans anyway. Despite his pleas, no one from the Family visited him or posted his bail. Worse, members of his own crew were suspiciously murdered while they were gathering money to secure his release. Feeling betrayed and with no one else to turn to, Barboza agreed to cooperate with the FBI.

Joe "The Animal" was now on the payroll and the 1960s had plenty of other curveballs for Raymond. He had been dealing with his wife's cancer diagnosis throughout the decade and in 1965, one of his oldest right-hand-men, Louis "The Fox" was indicted for tax evasion, convicted in 1967, and finally shot dead in front of his home in 1970. But before the new decade dawned, Raymond's worst fears had already come true. Teresa did a lot of damage, and Barboza did too when he flipped and ultimately testified, but the "witness" that Raymond couldn't kill proved most destructive at all. His fears of surveillance and wiretaps were justified and, as it turns out, Raymond's decision to cease all meetings at The Office in Providence was a decision made much too late.

CHAPTER 4
THE 1970S, FROM BEHIND BARS

In 1967 it was discovered that for months, the once-revered office of Raymond Patriarca, a room that had literally become synonymous with the New England Mafia itself, was riddled with FBI recording devices. During this period, nearly every conversation Raymond had with associates, whether mundane or criminal, was being eavesdropped upon. This included explicit conversations with other top guys, including Henry Tameleo and Angiulo, about activities related to ongoing investigations. The fact that this had continued on for so long under Raymond's nose was, unsurprisingly, a source of intense embarrassment for the don. His reputation in the public eye had long since been tarnished, but after this, his status as New England's underworld kingpin was also called into question. With the help of these tapes (they were later found to be inadmissible in court, but the damage was already done), as well as the cooperation of Barboza, the law was rapidly preparing to make its move against Il Patrone and his multiple-state-wide empire. The start of the 1970s would be the start of yet another completely new chapter in Raymond's life as his empire threatened to come undone.

Facing Kennedy's Music

Back in 1966, a mob-connected bookie out of Providence by the name of Willie Marfeo was shot dead as he ate lunch at a restaurant that was walking distance from Raymond's office. Marfeo had run afoul with the Patriarca clan several times and had made plenty of enemies from years of dodging his debts. It's not clear exactly who killed Marfeo, nor who gave the order, but it could have been any number of people in Rhode Island. Tameleo was suspected by some of Willie's brothers, and some suspected Barboza. This was a problem for Barboza as he was already worried about being gunned down every time he left his house, plus the Marfeos were, by all accounts, predictably violent. Luckily for him though, he had the FBI on his side and when it came time to prosecute for the murder, he was more than willing to point the finger in any and all directions. In 1969, Raymond Patriarca, Henry Tameleo, and Jerry Angiulo were all forced to defend themselves against the charges levied against them by mob informant Joe Barboza as he accused them all of orchestrating Marfeo's death.

The investigations didn't stop at Marfeo. The FBI was attempting their grand slam and successive charges would help pin down the Providence and Boston crews before they could weasel out of the consequences once again. After Marfeo, it was the murder of the Irish gangster and Bonanno Family associate Teddy Deegan that Barboza and his handlers in the FBI tried to throw at the Patriarcas. Deegan, who operated largely in the small and compact Massachusetts town of Chelsea, had started to become a growing figure in the Boston scene, and so his murder provided a good opportunity to strike at several of the top guys outside of Rhode Island. Tameleo was once again charged with murder, along with Peter Limone, Louis Greco, Ronnie Cassesso, Joe Salvati, and Willie

French. Barboza's testimony against them was damning but in reality, he was only actually aware of the involvement of Cassesso and French (ironically, Barboza himself was also involved in the Deegan hit). By the time Barboza and the federal agents guiding him were finished embellishing and outright lying their way through the court proceedings Tameleo, Limone, Greco, and Cassesso had received sentences of death. The other two were spared execution, but were sentenced to prison cells for the rest of their lives. As for Raymond, the Marfeo case resulted in a sentence of up to 10 years in prison, which is how he began the new decade. The upper echelon of Patriarca leadership had been decimated.

To illustrate the desperation that must have been felt by the Patriarca brass during the trial, one need only look to their defense's strategy in court. Raymond's last-ditch plan was, literally, to make Barboza so angry that he would physically assault them in court. Using potentially fabricated evidence gathered by a private investigator that Raymond hired, the defendants planned to accuse Barboza, among other things, of being a pimp, a drug mule, and of being the son of a prostitute. Everyone knew that Joe "The Animal" was notoriously hot-headed and ideally, an emotional or violent outburst from him would call into question his character and reliability before the jury. If nothing else, it would at least make a brand new trial necessary, thus extending their days as free men a little bit longer.

If Barboza's prior fear of being murdered was unwarranted, it wasn't any longer. The outrage throughout the New England mob against Joe was severe both during the trials and after they concluded. Generally speaking, lawyers were off limits when planning hits, regardless of who they represented. For Barboza, though, they were willing to make an exception. Sometime before the sentences from the Marfeo and Deegan cases were handed down, a car bomb was planted in the car of J. E. Fitzgerald, the man representing Barboza. It detonated as planned and cost the lawyer his leg, but he managed to at least survive the blast. Barboza was clearly a target though, and it had already been clear that he would need to be placed in witness protection at the conclusion of his service as state witness. With Jerry Angiulo being one of the few higher-ups in the Family to make it through Barboza's assault relatively unscathed, it was up to him to lead the unsuccessful hunt to kill the rat Barboza. Unsuccessful, that is, until 1976 when Joe "The Animal" became the first known man to be murdered while under federal witness protection after Jerry's connections learned where he was hiding out in California. In mid-February of that year, Barboza was shot dead and finally put out of his misery.

The entire Barboza situation caused intense stress throughout the high ranks of the Family. It caused members to turn on each other, especially Henry Tameleo, who had apparently been one of Joe's biggest defenders early on and had vouched for him on multiple occasions. Now though, in Tameleo's eyes he was a "weak, dirty piece of garbage," (quoted in Songini, 2015). Still, many—including Raymond—put at least partial blame for the entire situation on Tameleo, claiming that if not for Tameleo's recklessness and poor judgment of character, Barboza never would have been able to be linked to the Family anyway. Angiulo too blamed Tameleo for being the one who talked him down when he originally planned on killing Barboza some time earlier. Regardless of whether all this is completely true, the Family was distressed and needed someone to point the finger at. During and after the Barboza fiasco, the upper tier of the Family began efforts to try to weed out and eliminate any other possible informants hiding among them to avoid a repeat of the situation. The efforts were ultimately in vain, but much time was spent devising ways to identify the rats. This included starting a controlled disinformation campaign, whereby Raymond and the other high-ranking made guys would supply individual members and associates with random, contradictory pieces of information regarding criminal activity. Then, when being questioned or in conversation with the police or federal agents, it would be a simple matter of listening to what the officers accused them of, and then cross-referencing that with whom in the Family they gave that false information—then they would then have their man. It was a solid plan in theory, if a bit risky. Still, the Mafia's informant problem was not going away anytime soon, despite their best efforts.

While Raymond was in prison, he remained the official boss and continued to administer Providence, relaying his orders to his underlings from behind bars while Jerry Angiulo manned the Boston crews. Raymond at least managed to control his violent temper long enough for it to be considered "good behavior," and he ended up serving only about five years of his decade-long sentence. Still, it was a challenging period for him, and nearly everything about running a Family was made more difficult while in custody. Challenging, but not impossible. Several other bosses have done it, including Lucky Luciano and Vito Genovese, and Patriarca would do it too. While he was away though, a new and brutal figure was on the rise in Boston—the legendary Irish-American gangster Whitey Bulger. He caused problems for a lot of people as he led a bloody war through the streets of Boston, and Angiulo was one of them. Around the same time, a Patriarca associate named Stephen Flemmi began working with Bulger. Flemmi had a sour history with the Patriarcas, as Raymond once had to call a meeting with him to demand that he stop carrying out hits without permission from The

Office. Unbeknownst to Raymond, he had also been an informant for the FBI since at least the mid-1960s.

More than one disreputable FBI agent had a hand in all that had transpired in the Family during these years. In Barboza's case, it was his handlers Paul Rico and Dennis Condon who guided Joe through his various false testimonies, and Rico watched silently as The Animal perjured himself, under his own direction, in federal court. Rico was also aware of the Fitzgerald car bombing from the late '60s, and it was he who ensured Vincent Flemmi (Stephen's brother) fled while the investigation took place and saw to it that Frankie Salemme was fingered for it instead. In the case of Bulger and Stephen Flemmi, it was agent John Connolly pulling the strings (or, according to Bulger, perhaps it was the other way around). After Connolly met with the two gangsters and formed their initial understanding, Bulger and the Winter Hill Gang wreaked havoc with a renewed sense of impunity. Connolly was constantly running interference for Bulger's crew, even against other FBI agents, and served as his protector. With Connolly, whom Bulger referred to as "Zip," in their pocket, Angiulo's work was cut out for him. A staggering number of rival gangsters were massacred in Boston's streets during these years, including Joe Notarageli and Spike O'Toole, both of whom were murdered in 1973, as well as Tommy King two years later. Connolly was aware of the majority of these murders either before or after they happened, and he held Bulger and Flemmi responsible for exactly none of them. Rico and Connolly turned out to be borderline criminals themselves and, as we'll see, the law eventually came to recognize that.

Angiulo didn't have a ton of time to deal with the Winter Hill Gang and their violence in his city anyway. He had to prevent the Boston faction from falling out of line and rebelling in the absence of Il

Patrone, whose influence from prison was distant enough in Providence, let alone Massachusetts. To this end, Jerry appointed Ilario "Larry" Zannino, a Patriarca *caporegime*, to be his trusted number two in Beantown. Needing a trustworthy and reliable counsel, he also made his older brother and Patriarca veteran Nicolo Angiulo his *consigliere* in 1974. Acquiring a cool and level-headed advisor was wise, as just two years prior in 1972, Jerry inexplicably risked it all over what could have been a non-issue. Off the coast near the Boston Harbor in July of that year, the Coast Guard patrol identified and attempted to stop Angiulo while he was sailing around on his yacht. He could have cooperated and faced no consequences (there was apparently nothing illegal onboard that day), but he instead chose to sail his yacht away for miles, pretending like he didn't notice the Coast Guard ship attempting to hail him down. When he finally yielded and parked his boat near Dorchester, he proceeded to assault the officers attempting to board. When it was all said and done, Jerry had his day in court but only spent a month in jail, continuing his incredible streak of good luck.

In 1974, things were beginning to look relatively back to normal—the heat from the Barboza case and the car bombing was dying down, operations in Boston were continuing despite Bulger's rampage, and the Family was preparing to welcome back its long-time don, Raymond Patriarca, from his latest prison stint.

Patriarca Returns

In 1974, Raymond once again left his cell in Atlanta. He was a free man and was aiming to keep it that way, but he still had scores to settle. Upon his release, Patriarca was incensed at developments in the Mafia world. The rats, both Joe Barboza and Vincent Teresa, had authored expository books about their lives in the New England Patriarca Family which promised to be exclusive "tell-all" accounts. Several of these were published while Raymond was imprisoned, and some hit stores soon after his release, as though to pour salt in his fresh wounds. The real Mafia secrets that the two had exposed definitely would've angered Raymond, but likely far more annoying were the myriad fabrications and outright lies that they had put to their pages. Raymond had always disliked both of them (he reportedly hated Barboza) but now he wanted them dead. Teresa got off lucky and lasted until 1990 before dying of organ failure, but it took under three years to locate and murder Barboza. Joe Russo (not to be confused with the Colombo Family *capo* Joe Russo), a mobster with ties to both the Patriarca and Lucchese Family in NYC, tracked him down to San Francisco with Salemme. Suspecting the former enforcer would likely still be armed while under witness protection and a fake name (they were correct), Russo snuck up behind him to perform the execution.

So, Raymond was out of prison and the centerpiece of the prosecution that helped put him there had been repaid with several shotgun shells in the back. But not all was well in Providence, nor Boston. Raymond was now going to be under intense legal scrutiny for the remainder of his life, a fact that he understood painfully well even before his release. A perpetually stressed man, it wasn't long before his health began to decline. Accusations of misdoings continued to nag him, and in 1978 Teresa decided to speak up once again (he had already testified in 1971 and was responsible for several other made guys and associates being put away). This time, he divulged Raymond Patriarca's involvement in a bizarre, clandestine scheme orchestrated by the CIA to enlist American mafiosi in an attempt to assassinate Fidel Castro, the leader of Cuba.

Oddly enough, this wasn't the strangest route the CIA took to try to unseat the communist Caribbean President, but it was probably the most offensive to the American legal system. In any case, the ill-conceived plot was abandoned before it took off, but it would have made sense for both parties. When Castro took over in 1959, he led a mostly successful drive to eliminate the considerable influence of the American Mafia on the island and as a result, Families (including the Patriarcas) lost out on the lucrative Cuban gambling market. It's been alleged that part of the deal included a promise of safe haven for the Mob to operate in post-Castro Cuba. None of it came to fruition (including *any* of the attempts on Castro's life) but Patriarca's name was dragged through the national mud once again.

In 1981, things also started to really go downhill for Angiulo in Boston. That year, Whitey Bulger and Stephen Flemmi offered to draw up an accurate floor plan of Jerry's office on Prince Street and another on Margin Street for the FBI. Along with this, they would outline the best places for their handlers to install listening devices and wiretaps based on where they knew the Angiulo brothers typically discussed business. This allowed the two Winter Hill gangsters' handlers to infiltrate and thoroughly bug the Boston underboss' hideout. Listening intently, the federal agents got a solid three months' worth of recordings which they could sit on for a while to determine how best to use it against the Patriarcas. A number of high-ranking guys including Angiulo and Zannino had their voices identified on the tapes, once again discussing criminal activity and matters relating to ongoing investigations. It's somewhat surprising that Angiulo had allowed this to happen, considering he was well aware that the feds were eyeing his spots—Connolly's colleague Dennis Condon had frequently taunted Jerry by openly surveilling him at his office for years. Regardless, it happened; and among other things, authorities learned from Ilario Zannino's mouth that it was Russo who carried out the hit on Barboza back in 1976. Russo eventually went down for the hit (he was on the lam for some time under Raymond's orders to avoid being picked up for the shooting), but Angiulo was marked too.

In 1983 the FBI made their move on the Boston crime lord, arresting him on a multitude of charges including extortion, gambling, general racketeering, and ordering killings. His Mafia career and the entire Boston faction of the empire were now in jeopardy and Raymond feared losing yet another of his top guys. Despite attempting countless times to convince the judge and jury that he had been set up by Connolly and his Winter Hill stooges, Angiulo received a sentence so severe that, at his current age, he would have been about 112 years old upon his eventual release. The 45-year term was handed down to him in 1986 but before he served half of it, he was released due to poor health and died a couple years later. The Patriarca veteran appears to have been fully removed from operations in Boston post-1986. In the same trial, Jerry's right-hand man Zannino was also handed a conviction, along with several of his brothers. The North End crew was left emaciated and disorganized, a shell of its former self. With their main roadblock removed, Bulger and the Winter Hill Gang, with the help and oversight of Connolly, swept through the Boston scene to seize its rackets. The Italian gangs apparently never stood a chance without Angiulo and his crew in command.

While the legal battle with the Boston faction was underway, Raymond was dealing with his own charges in Providence. Back in 1965, Raymond had personally hired a hitman to gun down a petty street thug named Ray Curcio. Curcio, apparently desperate for cash, had broken into and robbed the house where Patriarca's son,

Junior, lived. Some sources, including the *New York Times*, reported at the time that it was actually Raymond's brother's house, which could have been the case considering Junior was just about 20 years old at the time. In any case, Raymond managed to avoid the consequences of this hit when he went to prison in 1969/70, but it had now come back to bite him. Witnesses in tow, the feds charged Raymond with the Curcio murder in 1983, and the next year, he was charged with yet another murder. This time it was the 1968 hit on Robert Candos, a known heister and associate that Patriarca reportedly believed was going to flip and turn witness. The feds were put onto Raymond's trail after the October 1980 arrest of Nicky Palmigiano, an associate of the Patriarcas, for firearm possession. Apparently Palmigiano claimed that he personally murdered both Curcio and Candos, and he was the one who initially fingered Raymond for ordering both of the hits. Raymond had been free for almost a decade, but the entire time likely felt very much like he was still in prison. Now, he risked going back for real. The process of preparing to defend himself once again, combined with the stress of having to try to manage affairs both at home in Providence and in out-of-state Boston was the final straw for Raymond. The two charges against him might as well have been a thousand charges—he would never end up facing the court for any of them.

CHAPTER 5

JUNIOR TAKES THE REINS

When Raymond Patriarca went away in 1970 for the Marfeo murder, his son Raymond Patriarca Jr. was only about 25 years old. Junior was involved in the Family's activities (although allegedly this was in spite of Raymond Sr.'s initial intentions) but was obviously too young to be given charge of Providence's rackets while the don was in prison. During this time it's not exactly clear what his role would have been, but he managed to climb the ladder enough during the 1970s that he became the heir apparent to his father's empire. The only problem was that, by all accounts, his rise was largely a result of Mafia nepotism. Junior appeared to have been ill-suited for mob life and was considered incompetent by more than a few of Providence's gangsters. Based on what he did in his later years after a stint in prison, it doesn't seem like he much considered himself a Mafia "lifer" anyway. According to a Connecticut attorney named Stanley A. Twardy Jr., "there was no reason to believe Raymond Patriarca [Jr.] was not in control of the Family, although there were certain indications he was not devoting all of his energies to running the Family," (quoted in Foderaro, 1989). Indeed, he may have been more of an "armchair boss." But, while many of his Family's top men, including his father, were facing potential legal action in the 1980s, Junior managed to avoid the vast majority of the heat. This put him in a good position to lead a potentially decimated Mafia clan in a worst-case scenario. With his father in poor health and facing a potential life sentence, this opportunity was rapidly approaching.

Gone for Good

In July of 1984, while both he and Jerry were being bombarded with accusations and charges, 76-year-old Raymond Patriarca Sr. suffered a heart attack. He was taken to a Rhode Island hospital where Judge McOsker decided to arraign him as he lay infirm in his hospital bed. The legal system was chugging along as though nothing had happened, but Raymond soon died while being treated. Just two years later, Angiulo was put in prison for good along with many others. According to Songini, "the New England Mafia became a walking corpse whose decay became more obvious every year," (2015). Still, the Mafia couldn't just dissolve, and the organization would need a new leader. The breakdown of the connection between Boston and Providence had unfortunately resulted in a considerable power struggle in the wake of Raymond's death, with one side backing Junior as the natural heir and the other supporting the highly-compromised Jerry Angiulo. It was lucky for Junior that although the Patriarca Family had lost its namesake, his last name still carried weight. Junior enjoyed widespread support in the underworld and the majority of the Providence faction was behind him. In New York, he received support from the Five Families, particularly the Colombos. Even Angiulo's own legally-embattled underboss threw his weight behind Junior for the boss position. Jerry with his crumbling power base in Massachusetts was unable to seize control of the entire operation, and eventually the New York Families stepped in to end the dispute. On a vote, the

Mafia Commission elected to cement Junior Patriarca in his father's former role.

Between the two, it was a beneficial decision for the Family. There was a sense of continuity even though Junior simply couldn't command the respect his father did, and as we know, Jerry Angiulo didn't have a lot of time left as a free man anyway. After his conviction, it's been reported that he was actually demoted or removed officially from the Family, likely as a result of his power grab. Being generally opposed to Junior's rise to boss, his veteran counsel probably couldn't be relied on anyway. Apparently, even after his imprisonment, Angiulo was making half-hearted attempts for a while to wrest and maintain control over Boston, none of which were successful. Even Larry Zannino, one of Jerry's top guys, ended up supporting Junior's bid after he himself briefly tried to consolidate power under him. Zannino was also headed to prison soon anyway on a 30-year sentence and, like Jerry, this was basically his death sentence. While his legal fate was still being decided, Larry was serving as the Commission-appointed *consigliere* to Junior in an effort to cool tensions between the now-distant Providence and Boston factions. Another pointless endeavor, as seeking advice and guidance on criminal matters from a man in federal custody proved virtually impossible. With Angiulo and Zannino put away in 1986, control over what remained seems to have been taken by Frank Salemme, who happened to be close associates with members of the Winter Hill Gang, notably Whitey Bulger and Flemmi. The fact that these two friends of his had been informing on his organization for roughly a decade was unknown to Salemme at the time.

Things in Providence weren't developing very smoothly either. It was quickly becoming clear to many that Junior was a Patriarca in name only and that his ability to maintain his father's Family was questionable. There were also a lot of issues with his public image. That, at least, he had in common with his father. But unlike Raymond Patriarca Sr., who only acquired his notoriety later in his life, Junior was already well-known, and he didn't exactly try to be discreet. He was known to call in to Rhode Island radio shows and happily announce who he was, always proud to play up the fact that he was the son of Il Patrone. He even partially owned a local restaurant that was clearly Mafia-themed. Needless to say, Junior's illicit ties to the underworld were a little "on the nose." He also didn't have the social clout that his father had earned from his years of philanthropy and charitable works in Providence and his area in particular. Raymond was known to favor those less fortunate than himself, often funding the school tuition for neighborhood youths, paying medical bills on behalf of struggling families, and donating to various causes and funds in the city. Though Raymond eventually had to cease his philanthropy when Family business started to take a severe downturn in the late 1960s and 1970s, the goodwill he had built up was apparently squandered with Junior in charge.

It was becoming clearer all the time that Junior's time atop New England's gangster totem pole was going to be a short-lived one. Most of the veteran mobsters who had been around for decades and had somehow managed to avoid prison believed Junior was a misguided choice in the first place. After all, Junior simply didn't have the upbringing nor the life experiences that Raymond Sr. did. Il Patrone, like most Mafia veterans, grew up poor and had to claw their way up from virtually nothing. It was survival of the fittest where only the most capable were able to survive and thrive. This, it was believed, developed the kind of character that was necessary to become a successful boss in La Cosa Nostra. Junior, on the other hand, grew up as the son of one of the most successful and powerful criminal kingpins on the eastern seaboard. He grew up in affluence in a safe, wealthy community, as opposed to a poor Italian ghetto, and was at least partially educated—a rare quality in the Mafia underworld. Most importantly, Junior was a part of that generation of mafiosi that came into their own in the post-Valachi period. The Mafia was already exposed, the code of honor and *omerta* that held the Mafia together for decades had dissolved, and it had become commonplace to save oneself by ratting on your friends. It seems that, despite their support for Junior's leadership bid, even the New York Families did not have much faith that the younger Patriarca would last very long.

Junior's Downfall

In the wake of Junior's ascension, it was William Grasso, known as "the Wild Man" or "Wild Guy Grasso," who was chosen to serve as the Patriarca underboss. The circumstances around Grasso's selection aren't known for sure, but it's possible that the decision emanated from New York City. Grasso was a Connecticut-based gangster who operated mostly out of Hartford. This was an area that was under the influence of both the Patriarcas and the Five Families and as such, Grasso ran his rackets for a long time as a member of the Colombo Family, who operated with the blessing of the New England Mafia. It wasn't an obvious choice for Grasso to take over underboss duties from Connecticut, but it's been suggested that one or more New York Families arranged for Grasso to be appointed so that he could oversee operations in Providence. Assuming the leadership in New York doubted Junior's capabilities, this would have made sense. With the Boston crew in shambles and the Irish

Winter Hill gang threatening to fully take over the Mafia's rackets there, they needed a more firm grasp on their out-of-state operations.

It was assumed for a long time that "Wild Guy" Grasso was, effectively, the don. It may have been the sort of situation where Junior functioned as more of a figurehead, which was not at all uncommon in the Mafia world, especially in the 1980s and 1990s. This was the era of RICO suits and witness hunting, and so many Families, notably the Genoveses, employed "front bosses," which were individuals meant to be seen as the boss in order for the real boss to operate outside of police scrutiny. Front bosses would be the ones to meet with other made guys and function as the mouthpiece for the real boss, who would rarely expose himself by discussing Family business anywhere besides the most secure locations. Junior would have made for a good front boss, as he drew plenty of police attention, took little issue with people associating him with the Mafia, and literally shared his name with Rhode Island's former public enemy number one. William Grasso, by comparison, was an unknown entity. If this truly was the strategy being used, it was at least partially effective: rival gangsters would get to Grasso well before the law was close to zeroing in on him.

It's impossible to say for sure what degree of control Grasso had over Junior and the Patriarca clan in the years he functioned as underboss from Hartford, but whatever the case was, it's clear that Junior was not regarded as a powerful or intimidating boss. This was true of both his friends and his many enemies, but it was apparently true of law enforcement as well. Even in Connecticut, authorities had long assumed that Grasso was the head honcho of the entire New England operation, which was made clear in the trial of Louis Failla, a low-level soldier of the lesser-known Connecticut faction of the Family. Failla was facing racketeering charges with seven other co-defendants, but Failla was also being charged with conspiracy to commit murder. Apparently he was given orders to murder Tito Morales, the father of Failla's grandson who had apparently run afoul with the Family. It was apparently an open-and-shut case, as Failla's vehicle had been bugged. Embarrassingly, Failla's hoarse, highly distinguishable voice was recorded specifically planning Morales' murder. Not only that, he also was heard bragging about his various illegal operations and rackets, and, inexplicably, even began rattling off the names of various other Patriarca members and associates who he conducted illegal business with. All the while, the prosecutors had been attempting to link Failla's criminal enterprise to William "The Wild Guy" Grasso, and *not* Raymond Patriarca Jr.

In the mid-1980s the FBI had plants everywhere, in various locations and in various ranks of the Mafia. They knew well the kind of reputation that Junior had and the lack of esteem that his fellow mobsters had for him, especially those located outside Rhode Island. In Boston especially, many within the remnants of the former Angiulo crew had grown bitter and resentful toward Junior's appointment as boss—many of the senior members in Boston who had initially supported Junior had since been put in prison. The FBI, still not finished with the Family, sought to exploit the perceived personal weaknesses of Junior Patriarca and explored ways to destroy the New England Mafia from within. In combination with legal prosecution, rattling the cages of the Family leadership would make them more vulnerable, sloppy, and less able to conduct their business. So, the feds began a campaign to sow discontent throughout the ranks of the Family, specifically among those who were less than satisfied with Junior as boss. Using state boundaries to their advantage, they focused their efforts on Massachusetts and Connecticut-based gangsters.

Central to the FBI's plan was the effort by both federal agents and their plants, namely Angelo Mercurio, to convince Patriarca Family members and associates that Junior was preparing to take action against them. Mercurio, nicknamed "Sonny," ended up having nearly as destructive an impact on the New England Mafia as Joe "The Animal" Barboza had years earlier. He was a Boston native who grew up just outside the city and, born in 1936, he was about 9 years older than Junior. Since even before he was confirmed to be associated with the Patriarcas, Mercurio had an impressive rap sheet. At just 18 years old, a Massachusetts judge handed him a sentence of life imprisonment for his role in an armed robbery just outside Boston. That could have been the end of the story, and the Patriarcas would have been better off, but fate once again stepped in. Mercurio received a pardon from the state after about 10 years and was a free man in 1964, the same year Barboza got out. During this time, he definitely became associated with the Patriarcas, if he wasn't already. The problem was that he was also closely associated with the Winter Hill Gang, and often served as a middleman in their dealings during the late 1960s and 1970s.

As it turns out, Mercurio flipping was in itself a payoff of the efforts of the FBI in Boston to recruit from within. When Sonny was sent away on another prison bid around 1978, the Family was already suffering deeply and had been basically forsaking anyone who was unlucky enough to be put away. This meant that even made guys who were in prison often got little support from the Family. In Sonny's case, no one was collecting from his operations on his behalf and his family reportedly didn't see a dime from any Patriarca members while he was incarcerated. The resentment that this bred was fueled by the Winter Hill Gang, whose members Whitey Bulger and Stephen Flemmi made sure his loved ones were taken care of. When Mercurio was out in 1986, he was one of the clearest examples of mafiosi who were dissatisfied with Junior, and this made him an easy target for Connolly and his stooges to manipulate. So, at some point after his release (around 1986 or 1987), Flemmi provided yet another floorplan to Connolly, this time of the basement of Sonny's Italian grocery store in the Prudential Center on Boston's Boylston Street. Once they had enough dirt on Mercurio to get a likely conviction, they charged him with extortion and racketeering. Facing another term in prison, he was presented with the option of instead cooperating and informing on the Patriarcas, which Flemmi coaxed him into accepting. In 1987, Mercurio became the latest Patriarca on the FBI's payroll. Together, Mercurio, Winter Hill, and the feds began causing unrest within the ranks, which included convincing them that Junior was currently planning a purge of the Family and would soon make moves on those he believed were disloyal or otherwise unhappy with his leadership. Chaos soon followed, and this strategy proved to be effective in the coming years.

The 1980s had three more major challenges in store for the Patriarcas before the decade closed, at least two of which Mercurio had a hand in. In June of 1989 Frank Salemme, who had been climbing the Patriarca ranks for years, was advised by Mercurio to attend a sit-down (if you can call it that—it reportedly took place in an IHOP parking lot) between high-ranking members of the now-feuding Providence and Boston factions. Specifically, Salemme was in a struggle with Joe Russo, who was supported by Mercurio, and both of them were reportedly vying for control. Unfortunately for "Cadillac Frank," Sonny's meeting was a setup. As he awaited the other supposed attendants, armed men approached him unseen and fired. Salemme caught two bullets, one in the lower body and another in his chest, though it luckily avoided his heart. Wounded, he frantically shambled into the restaurant and then out through its back entrance as his would-be assassins continued to unload before fleeing the scene. Salemme ultimately survived but he and his crew were shaken, and the bad blood only got worse.

Then, the same month that Frank was very nearly whacked, Junior's underboss "Wild Guy" Will Grasso was murdered. He was shot at close range while en route to Worcester, where he planned to attend to business regarding the remnants of Raymond Patriarca's old Coin-O-Matic vending operation. The shooter was presumably the only passenger known to be in the car with him at the time, Gaetano Milano, a made guy from Springfield, MA. Grasso's body was eventually recovered, floating down the Connecticut River near Hartford, and Milano was later picked up for the murder. When defending himself, Milano claimed that the murder was necessary self-defense, as the Patriarca Family was in a be-or-be-killed situation where everyone was at each other's throats. Believing that Grasso, the force behind Junior, was soon going to make his move against disloyal elements in the Family, Milano apparently was forced to act first. Clearly, the campaign by Mercurio, Flemmi, Bulger, and the FBI to spread suspicion and violent mistrust was proving to be a resounding success. With these new developments, different factions of the Family began fighting each other more aggressively for dominance and with Grasso gone and Junior weaker than ever, the young boss could not hope to maintain his position. While we don't know if Mercurio had *directly* contributed to the hit on Grasso, his role in the third and final disaster of 1989 was essential.

CHAPTER 6
DISCONTENT IN THE COMMONWEALTH

Needless to say, the 1980s were not friendly to the Patriarca Family. Infighting, treachery, and greed had crippled the connection that once bound the cities of Providence and Boston and as a result, the Family's operation was hobbled. Aside from the murders and murder attempts, the 1980s was also the era of the "crack epidemic" moral panic. Americans in cities across the country were becoming more afraid of the effects of drug abuse and of drugs entering their communities and as a result, the so-called war on drugs was revitalized. Along with that came far more severe punishments for both drug possession and drug distribution. In New England, the Mafia controlled a large portion of both the cocaine and cannabis market, which state and federal law enforcement began to crack down hard on in the 1980s. This, combined with the fact that most dealers in the Mafia were also strung out on their own drugs, made drug peddlers easy targets for witness hunting. The crusade against the drug rackets in New England continued to plague the Patriarcas well into the 1990s, but it still did not have the destructive power of Angelo Mercurio's final backstab. Rather than Family *capos* and underlings, his target this time was Junior Patriarca himself.

Junior's Last Straw

In the 1980s, the Patriarcas' long-standing political and judicial connections began to fall apart. One of the most notable of Raymond's old connections was Joseph Bevilacqua, the former Speaker of the Rhode Island House of Representatives and later Chief Justice of the state's Supreme Court. Bevilacqua, who was born in Providence in 1918, was apparently a close friend of Raymond Sr. for years, and in 1973—one year before Patriarca was released from prison—Bevilacqua testified to his supposedly impeccable moral character and unshakable integrity. There's little doubt that Bevilacqua was a considerable influence in the Parole Board's decision to release Raymond Sr. before his sentence had been fully served (Bevilacqua's connections didn't stop at Raymond Sr.; he was apparently close with the veteran Nick Bianco as well). Politically speaking, his praise of a well-known criminal and accused murderer was certainly a strange move that earned suspicious glances from more than a few of his colleagues. In fact, by the time Bevilacqua was elected to the office of Chief Justice, his connections to Italian-American organized crime were so well-known that he felt obligated to publicly denounce his past and assure his colleagues that he had already moved on from it. However, this was clearly not true, and it became obvious by the early 1980s. He had been identified visiting the homes of known Patriarca Family members several times, was accused of allowing criminals to hide in his home in return for cash payments, and was known to be an avid customer of the Patriarca Family's prostitution establishments. By 1984 he was under intense scrutiny and two years later he was impeached. Bevilacqua resigned from office in 1986, and thus the Patriarcas had lost a vital piece of their legal advantage. The Family could no longer rely on Rhode Island's Chief Justice to run interference for them.

Junior's position was now tenuous, at best. Many rival gangsters wanted to unseat him by force if necessary, and most who didn't directly oppose him still believed that he should probably be removed. The last straw for him came later in 1989 at—of all things—a Mafia induction ceremony; the secretive rites that Joe Valachi had exposed decades earlier. Some time before the ceremony took place, Mercurio tipped off Connolly as to its date and whereabouts. This gave them time to form a plan, and Mercurio ended up agreeing to wear a listening device on his person while he attended the induction in Medford. When the time came, Sonny dutifully concealed the wire and made sure to stand as close as he could to whoever was talking to get the clearest sound quality. The entire hours-long ceremony was recorded, along with the identifiable voices of the roughly dozen mobsters who were attending including Junior, Joe Russo, Nick Bianco, Matt Guglielmetti, Vincent Ferrara, and even Bobby Carrozza, also known as "Baby/Bobby Russo," one of the leading figures behind the Patriarca rebellion. Junior's hobby of calling into popular radio shows and announcing himself came back to haunt him: cross-referencing his radio appearances with the recording made his voice particularly easy to identify. During the ceremony, Junior announced that Russo would be the new official head of the Boston faction, and then Russo carried out the induction rites, which included bloodletting, an oath of both silence and loyalty to the Family, and burning a picture of a Catholic saint while the initiate holds it. And the feds heard every word of it.

This scheme, made possible by the treachery of Mercurio, was the first time that a Mafia induction ceremony had been successfully bugged by the FBI. The most obvious repercussion of this historic bit of espionage was that now the government had undeniable proof that Junior, Russo, and others, were all a part of the same criminal organization, not to mention the brand new recruits Vincent Federico, Ricky Floramo, Rob DeLuca, and Carmen Tortora. This evidence would allow a potential future RICO suit against them to be far more effective. RICO suits, feared by the Mafia since their inception, stood for Racketeer Influenced and Corrupt Organizations. It was a sweeping reform in American criminal justice and allowed for the mass prosecution of an unlimited number of defendants in a criminal case. If one individual was charged with a crime and it was determined that that crime was performed in the service of a broader criminal organization, prosecutors were able to trace a line all the way up to the leader of the organization and charge every single person along the way, all for one criminal action. Further, it allowed federal agents to effectively cripple an organization before a court conviction or even a trial. If a RICO suit was launched and agents suspected that funds possessed by the accused were acquired illegally, the prosecution was allowed to freeze all of those assets, rendering the accused effectively poor. For example, if the government believed that a certain club owned by a Patriarca man was utilized in criminal dealings, assets and income related to the establishment could be seized before they even had a chance to defend themselves. So, with Mercurio's recording, the FBI's job was made very easy, as it was spelled out for them exactly who was in the organization as well as who the leaders were of both the Boston and Providence crews.

When the news broke that the ceremony, which had been approved and overseen by Junior, had been taped by the FBI, whatever respect that was still attached to Raymond Jr.'s last name had vanished along with any hopes he had of reforging his father's crumbling empire. It was a calamity for the entire Patriarca Family and an embarrassment for everyone involved in its planning, but ultimate blame was laid squarely at Junior's feet. The fact that he allowed a sacred Mafia tradition to be sloppily exposed by a rat wearing a hidden wire was beyond disgraceful, and Junior lost all ability to maintain control over his underlings and prevent the splitting of the Family. In addition, with the tape in the hands of the government and with plenty of investigations already ongoing, aggressive legal action was expected before long. Under these conditions, Junior had little choice but to step down as head of the Family. After only five years as don, Junior was out, with neither his tenure nor his legacy having even approached that of his father.

Yet again, the Family was in need of a new boss. Ultimately, the job fell to Nick Bianco, whether he wanted it or not. Interestingly, Bianco was actually the man that most expected would have taken the position of boss in the first place after Patriarca Sr.'s death, as he was respected and had significant ties to the Five Families in NYC. Born in Providence in 1932, Bianco was a venerable gangster whose roots dated back to Frank Morelli and the Morelli Brothers crew. Although he cut his teeth in Rhode Island, he was highly mobile, traveling frequently between his home state and New York where he formed lifelong connections, especially in Brooklyn. Having been associated with the Colombos since the days when they were known as the Profaci Family, he was considered a part of the old school and as such, he outclassed Junior in just about every category that mattered, except he didn't share the Patriarca last name. The popular yet unfulfilled expectation that Bianco would step into the role vacated by Raymond Sr. was not surprising, given that Bianco was asked to return to New England in the early 1970s by his friend

Joe Colombo in order to help maintain control while Il Patrone was serving his prison sentence. His time finally did come in 1989 but it was far too late to reverse any of the damage that had already been done—damage which Bianco may have had some outside chance at preventing had he been given control years earlier. Regardless, he didn't have much time left for any kind of course correction.

The Troublesome 90s

Some accounts claim that Nick Bianco was eventually selected to be Junior's successor because he was one of the few high-ranking members not present at the induction ceremony. Others claim that Bianco was in fact present, but he was selected because either he didn't speak, his voice wasn't identified, or because he simply managed to avoid the negative repercussions of the induction recording. In any case, Bianco was in and was cleared of suspicion, at least for the immediate term. Soon, likely as anticipated, the incident in Medford led to legal action against most of its participants, but the results were worse than expected. Junior, as well as nearly two dozen other members and associates, were hit with a plethora of charges in one of the largest single attacks on an organized crime Family in history. Junior was indicted on RICO charges in March of 1990, accused of, among many other things, interstate narcotics dealing, gambling, general racketeering, murder, and conspiracy to commit murder. After everything was said and done, Junior was sent to prison for eight years, which marked the end of his incredibly underwhelming career as a mobster. Even after his eventual release, he showed no signs of wanting to return to the Family he helped drive into the ground. The rest of the defendants, including Ferarra and Matt Guglielmetti, were also put away for years and received hefty financial penalties. Clearly, the Mafia was beginning the new decade with a whimper, not a bang.

The one saving grace of the Medford fiasco was that now, at least, the Family was under the leadership and guidance of a veteran elder statesman mafioso in Nick Bianco. Unfortunately, this wasn't meant to last, and Bianco's brief time as Providence kingpin would be over before he could accomplish anything meaningful. Later in 1990, Bianco was charged with fraud, racketeering, and conspiring to commit homicide. It was another RICO suit and Bianco, as well as numerous other associates, were facing long sentences and harsh fines. In 1991, Bianco was convicted. He was sent off to prison, right behind Junior Patriarca, for just over eleven years. The length of sentence didn't matter too much for Bianco though—within three years he died in prison from complications related to his recent diagnosis of Lou Gehrig's disease. The onslaught didn't stop at the group convictions of Junior and Bianco. In 1993, over 20 other Patriarca associates were hauled before federal court to defend themselves against charges of illegal bookie operations.

With Bianco unseated before he barely had a chance to sit down, the Patriarca power vacuum was opened once again. Frank Salemme, who was still attempting to run operations in Boston, made a bid for the boss position. At least in Massachusetts, Salemme had few rivals for power. He and his crew had the backing of the Winter Hill Gang, plus Bulger and Flemmi were more than willing to assist an ally in taking over the organization that once posed the greatest threat to them. With their support, Salemme became the next boss of the Patriarca family and for the first time since Raymond Patriarca Sr. took over in 1954, the seat of the Patriarcas' power was shifted back to Boston. Now, the three friends Bulger, Flemmi, and Salemme were in charge of two of the biggest criminal organizations in New England, and at least two of them had a working relationship with the FBI. Unfortunately though, Bulger's long-time FBI contact and handler John Connolly had retired by the mid-1990s. Apparently, with him went Bulger and Flemmi's protection.

In 1995, the criminal trio and three other associates were indicted with a total of 37 racketeering charges against them. Although Connolly couldn't stop the investigation or indictments, he did take a risk by at least letting Bulger know ahead of time that the indictments were coming, just in time for him to make himself scarce and abandon his comrades to the mercy of the law. After Bulger fled the state, Flemmi did not take over leadership of Winter Hill as might have been presumed, likely because it was almost inevitable that he'd be inside of a jail cell before long. Rather, control was given to Kevin Weeks, one of Bulger's closest friends and apprentices. Weeks was highly active in Winter Hill and helped the gang bring the city's drug industry under control in the 1980s. During this period, Winter Hill weren't so much drug *dealers* as they were drug enforcers—instead of selling cocaine and cannabis, Winter Hill simply threatened those who did with death if they refused to kick up to Bulger. Weeks served as the key street man in this operation, being the muscle that kept the city's dealers in line. Weeks was clearly of a rare breed of loyalty, as even after Bulger was running from the law, Weeks continued to wire him tens of thousands of dollars wherever he was, which Bulger then stored in various safes dotted around the country (soon though, Weeks' loyalty would be put to the ultimate test). Salemme, for his part, tried to flee as well but he was far less successful than Bulger, who managed to evade the law for the better part of two decades. Like Bianco, Salemme was hit with eleven years.

Before Salemme was put away though, it was already clear he, like Junior and Bianco, would not be able to prevent the Family's downfall. The infighting was still severe when he took over, and relatively petty offenses (or perceived offenses) were routinely escalating into nearly full-on Mafia civil wars. In 1994, a lowly Patriarca soldier Nino Cucinotta shot dead two of his fellow made guys, Pete Scarpellini and Ronnie Coppola, over a heated exchange during a card game. The same year, one of Frankie Salemme's narcotics guys was murdered over another trivial dispute. While all this was happening, Bulger was still running free across the city, backstabbing and double-crossing until he was forced to go on the lam. Salemme was soon headed on the lam as well though. In 1993 Steve DiSarro, the manager of a nightclub known to be frequented by local mafiosi (DiSarro himself had mob ties too) was murdered. Suspicion of informants lurking among the Mafia was running high by this point, and it's likely that the manager was murdered because he was suspected of cooperating with federal agents (all this was ironic for Salemme, whose closest associates had been rats for decades). Whatever it was that led to the hit on the manager, Salemme was suspected of ordering it. Once he caught wind that the hit was being investigated, he took off for Florida. Before long though, he was apprehended and brought right back. Salemme was off to prison, but his story did not end there like Junior's did. The Patriarca Family was on the precipice of facing a new, even darker chapter of their fall from power.

CHAPTER 7
COLLAPSE: THE MAFIA TODAY

By the mid-1990s and 2000s, the Mafia landscape all over the country had been irreparably altered. The "glory days" were long gone, and all the elder mafiosi could do was complain about the lack of values and respect that the new generation of gangsters seemed to have. In prior decades, prison was not something to be necessarily feared, but rather expected. If you got pinched and had to go to jail, you kept your mouth shut and went to prison. When you were released, things more or less went back to normal. By this new age, the prospect of facing prison time was enough to get the vast majority of mobsters to flip on even their closest friends. Ultimately though, blame for the collapse of the Mafia had more to do with the decision to actually treat organized crime as a threat to America. Their new and aggressive tactics, which had been in development since the mid-1960s, are mostly to blame for this state of affairs. It had put a rapid succession of Patriarca bosses (and other bosses for that matter) in prison, and it was clear that the days of venerable leaders naming Families after themselves and reigning for decades had long since died. Though even now the Mafia has still not been fully excised from American society, the 1990s turned them into the "walking corpses" that they remain today, desperately trying to earn illegal income wherever they can find it. If they could operate without violently turning on each other, that is.

Salemme and the Civil War

Interestingly, Salemme had Angelo Mercurio, the man who recorded the Medford initiation, to (partially) thank for his downfall. While Mercurio had been serving prison time for his participation in the attempted hit on Salemme during Carrozza's rebellion (for his work as an informant, he was serving a significantly reduced sentence), he was brought back into the FBI's service once more in the late 1990s. He was sent from his cell to another Boston court where he divulged everything he knew about Salemme's criminal enterprise. This was actually the first time Mercurio showed his face in court and outed himself as an informant—until now, the Family was unaware that he was the one wearing the wire—and as a result, he had to enter federal witness protection after he was released (his sentence was reduced yet again after his contributions toward convicting Salemme). Mercurio probably didn't feel as secure as he should have, considering Barboza was tracked down all the way on the other side of the country. Mercurio was either luckier than Barboza, or the Family was rendered so weak by the late 1990s that they simply didn't have the resources to search for him. In any case, Mercurio lived out the rest of his natural life, dying in 2006.

After Salemme was apprehended and brought before the courts along with Flemmi, the Family ranks were apparently at their wit's end. With yet another new boss facing RICO indictments and likely over a decade in prison, the rebellion that began years earlier under Bob Carrozza began to develop into a civil war that lasted until about 1997. The Family split into factions, one consisting of those who continued to support Salemme during and after his trial, and the other consisting of renegade Carrozza loyalists. These factions continued to trade blows for months and left plenty of victims dead in the process, including Richard DeVincent, unflatteringly known as "the pig," who was gunned down in 1996. But before the rebellion could get any bloodier, the FBI made their move. In mid-1997 federal agents swept through New England, specifically the Boston area, picking up over a dozen members of Carrozza's amateurish crew, including "Baby/Bobby Russo" and his top guys. This was good and bad for the Salemme faction. On the one hand, this effectively ended the civil war by decimating the rebellious element and locking up their leader. On the other hand, the FBI's reason for indicting Carrozza's faction was clear: they wanted more state witnesses to use against the Family (i.e., the remnants of Salemme's loyalists). Before everything was done, four of Carrozza's crew agreed to testify against the Family in return for a reduction or absolvement of their potential RICO sentences.

After Salemme's fate was sealed, Louis/Luigi Manochio, also known as "Baby Shacks," was next in line to take over. In a rare case, the Providence-based Manocchio managed to remain in power for quite some time, breaking the trend of recent Patriarca bosses. This was even more impressive considering his advanced age at the time—born in 1927, Manocchio was another veteran mobster who was earning his reputation while the likes of Junior Patriarca were still in elementary school. Still, Manocchio clearly wasn't anyone's first choice, considering he only rose to power after virtually every other capable leader in the Family had been under federal indictment. Still, it was Manocchio that guided the family through the rest of the 1990s, into the new decade and new millennium. Manocchio's record was far from spotless, and in 1996 he and others were charged in connection with various high-profile burglaries in the area. He was facing prison time, but eventually pleaded guilty to all charges in exchange for a three-year term of probation which he miraculously served without being picked up again.

The 2000s brought new challenges for most and new opportunities for some, including Frank Salemme. Having eventually issued a guilty plea for racketeering (the murder charge in the DiSarro case had been dropped in return for the plea and Salemme's assurance that he had nothing to do with it), Salemme was apparently not ready to spend the full eleven years in prison at his age. His way out was familiar—he would have to testify against his former Winter Hill friends and associates. With Manocchio attempting to calm the tensions amidst the Family, Salemme threatened to burn it all down again. Ultimately though, Salemme's bid for freedom worked and Manocchio continued as boss for nearly a decade into the 2000s.

The Patriarcas in the 21st Century

At some point while Frankie Salemme was serving his sentence for racketeering, likely around 1999 or 2000, the former boss finally became aware of the treachery of Whitey Bulger and Stephen Flemmi. Having learned that his close associates had been on the FBI's payroll since the days of Raymond Sr., Salemme was incensed. With the help of agent Connolly, his two Winter Hill associates had orchestrated the Patriarcas' downfall in Boston, all the while they ran their own operations with near-immunity. Initially refusing to turn witness, Salemme was now an eager state participant. He told his counsel that he would be willing to give any information he had, not only on the fugitive Bulger and the imprisoned Flemmi, but on their handler John Connolly as well. Based on his testimony, the government investigated the role that the FBI handlers had played in New England's organized criminal underworld. In addition to Salemme though, former Winter Hill leader Kevin Weeks also flipped while he was in prison for drug-related RICO charges. Apparently, his years of loyalty were destroyed by one conversation with an unnamed, disgruntled, imprisoned former member of the Patriarcas—he essentially told Weeks that he was a sucker for not cooperating because the guys he was protecting would have flipped on him in an instant. This was probably true, and Weeks knew it. From then on, Weeks gave the FBI everything he had on Flemmi, Connolly, and his own mentor Whitey Bulger. Years later, the retired John Connolly was set to face trial and with the assistance of Salemme, it was determined that Connolly was little more than a criminal himself. He was convicted and sent off to prison, put there by the same man he had put in prison years earlier. In exchange for this, Salemme was released from prison in 2003 and placed in witness protection. But at 70 years old, his story was *still* not completed, nor was his criminal record.

Connolly wasn't the only crooked federal agent to face consequences in the new millennium. Harold Paul Rico, the man responsible for handling Joe Barboza (among others), was also under federal scrutiny for his role in the late-1960s convictions of Henry Tameleo, Peter Limone, Louis Greco, Joe Salvati, Willie French, and Ronnie Cassesso. In 2001, four of these men were exonerated for their crimes as the government discovered that the testimony Barboza gave, where he alleged that the accused had ordered the killing of Edward Deegan, was falsified. Unfortunately, Louis Greco had died a few years earlier in 1995 and Tameleo was long gone, having died ten years before him. Limone and Salvati were more fortunate—both lived long enough to be released into society again, and each was awarded tens of millions of dollars in their wrongful conviction settlement. Two years later, former agent Rico was forced to defend himself against the accusation that he was the one who coaxed Barboza into pointing the finger at the Patriarca men (although it's likely that Barboza would have blamed the Patriarcas anyway considering his resentment toward them at the time), and that he obstructed justice by observing Barboza's court perjury and not bothering to report the crime. He was also indicted for instructing Bulger and Flemmi of Winter Hill to organize a hit in Oklahoma back in 1981. While imprisoned awaiting trial in 2004, Rico died at 78.

Back in Providence, where Luigi Manocchio once again rooted the Patriarca Family headquarters, things appear to have gone relatively smoothly for several years, at least for the boss. Little is known about this period of the Patriarca Family history, but we do know that the elderly Manocchio remained boss until 2009. The year before he stepped down, he was under investigation for suspected criminal activity taking place at several of his nightclubs. To avoid being fingered as the head of a multi-state criminal organization, he gave up the reins to Peter Limone, one of the men released from prison in 2001 after his conviction was overturned. At some point, Manocchio followed the footsteps of several New England gangsters before him and fled Rhode Island for Florida. It was here in the Sunshine State in 2011 that he was apprehended and charged with the extortion of two Providence strip clubs, the Cadillac Lounge on Charles Street and the Satin Doll Gentleman's Club on Aborn Street. The next year Manocchio pleaded guilty and was handed a five-and-a-half-year sentence. In 2013 the Satin Doll was fined and ordered to shut down by the city for allegedly operating a prostitution ring out of their private booths, which led the city administration to consider outlawing all private spaces in strip clubs. Manoccio was eventually released in 2015 before his sentence was completed. Having turned 96 years old in 2023, Manocchio currently lives as a free man.

Boston man Peter Limone had brought the operations back to Massachusetts once again, but his time as a free man lasted less than a year after Manocchio abdicated. Considering he refused to turn witness even after being handed a sentence for a crime he knew for a fact he didn't commit, it was unsurprising that the Family trusted Limone. Still, it was a strange decision for him to return to organized crime at all—he must have been extremely wealthy at this point, having been awarded $26 million himself due to his wrongful imprisonment (Gross, n.d.). Unfortunately he also had serious, new legal problems of his own, so his reign was ill-fated and tenuous from the beginning. Eventually charged with racketeering, he was handed a suspended sentence which meant that any more criminal wrongdoing would result in him dying in prison. It was a light sentence, but one that was warranted considering he already spent three decades in federal custody under false pretenses. The rest of the Family also took hits in these years, including *consigliere* Tony Parrillo, who was arrested for assault in 2011 and eventually sentenced to five years.

After Limone was forced to effectively halt his criminal dealings for the term of his probation, the younger DiNunzio brother, Anthony, became acting boss in his stead. Anthony's older brother, Carmen DiNunzio, had recently been sent away for five and a half years for attempting to bribe law officials. Anthony was headed to prison too before long. The younger DiNunzio had connections in the New York Gambino Family and together they had worked together to seize control of a large swathe of strip clubs in Providence and the surrounding area. The move unsurprisingly drew a lot of heat, all of which came down on him in 2012. He pleaded guilty and received six years in prison, meaning Antonio Spagnolo was next in line. In 2014, Spagnolo and fellow Patriarca member Pryce Quintina, both of whom were in their 70s at the time, were arrested and indicted on extortion charges related to gambling establishments in Boston. Likely due to their advanced age, neither were sent to prison but they were placed under house arrest and forced to wear location-tracking ankle bracelets, effectively eliminating Spagnolo's ability to run the Family.

Anthony DiNunzio's older brother Carmen, nicknamed "Cheese Man," was released from prison just in time to take over acting boss duties from the home-interned Antonio Spagnolo. Carmen, who was an old member of the Patriarcas' North End crew, immediately set out to solidify his position, considering the advanced age of boss Peter Limone at the time which suggested the Family would need a new official boss before long. He inducted a slew of new made guys into his crew, including his own nephew Louis, who earned the affectionate nickname "Baby Cheese," a nod to his uncle. In an effort to make the Boston base of operations more robust, DiNunzio promoted his close ally, the exceedingly overweight Greg Costa, to captain of the city's North End. Matthew Guglielmetti was installed as Carmen/Limone's underboss, and Joe Achille was made *consigliere*. Both Guglielmetti and Achille were long-time members of the Rhode Island crew, which signaled that the Patriarca Family Boston-Providence connection was not completely fractured, and in fact may have been recovering under Limone and DiNunzio. In 2017, boss Limone died, leaving Carmen to fully inherit the Patriarca clan. Later in 2020, Guglielmetti's health took a turn for the worse and he abdicated his position as underboss, which was then given to Eddie Lato. As far as we know, both Guglielmetti and Lato remain active in their positions today.

In 2018, former boss (and former FBI witness) Frank Salemme, who had been living under witness protection, was yet again coming under federal scrutiny. When he was initially sent to prison for racketeering charges years earlier, he had denied having anything to do with the disappearance of the mobbed-up nightclub manager Steven DiSarro. In 2015 William Ricci, who was associated with the Patriarca Family, was investigated for operating an illegal cannabis growing operation out of the apartment complex that he owned in Providence. During the course of the investigation, authorities received a tip that the building was concealing something more sinister. After a thorough search and digging around the property, authorities discovered DiSarro's decayed remains. The case, which was long assumed to be a homicide but technically considered to be a disappearance, was reopened. They turned their attention toward Salemme and in 2018 they hauled him into court once again.

At the time, Salemme was living under the assumed name "Richard Parker" in Atlanta, Georgia. When the news broke that DiSarro's remains were discovered and that Salemme was suspected, he fled witness protection and holed up in a hotel in Connecticut. Authorities discovered him there, along with tens of thousands of dollars in cash. Testifying against him were the DeLuca brothers, Joe and Bobby. Bobby was a former *caporegime* in the Family (he had also turned witness back in the mass prosecution of 2011), but Joe's standing is not known for certain. Joe told the court that back in 1993, Frank Salemme had contacted him to organize a meet-up and hand off a "package" to Joe. The pair met at a vacant parking lot in Providence and, according to the DeLucas, the "package" was Steven DiSarro's corpse, wrapped haphazardly in a tarp. Joe testified that he was the one who transported and disposed of DiSarro's body on Ricci's property under the direct orders of boss Frank Salemme. With these two star witnesses' testimonies, Salemme was eventually convicted of both DiSarro's murder and of perjuring himself in his trial several years prior when he feigned ignorance of the situation.

The official story was that Salemme's son, Frank Jr., committed the murder by strangling him to death while Patriarca associate Paul Weadick held him down and Salemme Sr. silently observed. Frank Jr. certainly would have faced trial alongside his father, but he had died in 1995. Salemme's defense attorney made unsuccessful efforts to call into question the integrity of those accusing Salemme, although he technically admitted that the mobster was a murderer. Hilariously, part of his defense strategy was to claim that although Salemme of course murdered people in the past, it doesn't mean he murdered *this* person: "Just because he's done these bad things doesn't mean he's done this," (quoted in Telford, 2018). Both 85-year-old Frank Salemme as well as Patriarca associate Paul Weadick were given life sentences in federal prison and Salemme died in 2022. Weadick, still alive as of the Summer of 2023, is reportedly seeking a new trial for his involvement.

The 2020s also saw more of the Patriarca's former political connections slip away. Deputy Chief of Staff John Conti was put under police surveillance in 2020 under suspicions that he was involved with a known associate of the Patriarcas, Ray Jenkins. Jenkins was known to be involved in a Rhode Island-based cannabis growing racket and Conti was suspected of being either involved or a direct partner in its operation. The surveillance effort was a success, and Conti was recorded associating with Jenkins. It was also revealed later that Conti had also met, on at least one occasion, with Patriarca underboss Matt Guglielmetti, which signals that Conti's ties were not only to low-level made guys and associates. Clearly it has become far more difficult to remain an organized criminal with political safety nets in the 21st century, but the fact that Conti only resigned as late as 2022 goes to show that the Patriarca Family still commands considerable power and influence in their home states, though the days of Raymond Patriarca Sr. supposedly dominating even the Five Families of New York City were very long gone, and that fact remains painfully obvious.

CONCLUSION

More than anything else, the story of the Italian Mafia's history in America is one of violence, betrayal, greed, and honor. Today, it is one of nostalgia—a longing for the "good old days" when mafiosi were seemingly untouchable, police officers and judges were easily plied, and the Mafia was something worth making films about. The general fascination with the glory days of the Mafia is born out of the success of cinematic masterpieces such as *The Godfather* and Martin Scorsese's *Goodfellas* and *Casino*. Francis Ford Coppola's *The Godfather,* which hit theaters in 1972 while the American Mafia was still very much a force to be reckoned with, portrays a highly romanticized version of the Mafia. Set in the 1940s and 1950s, it shows a period where honor, secrecy, and the sacred principle of *omerta* reigned. Unsurprisingly, it is typically this version of the Mafia that even mafiosi today look to as a model for how a Family *should* be run. It's actually an incredible reversal—once, filmmakers looked to the real-life Mafia to guide their vision on screen. Today, mobsters look to these landmark films for inspiration.

The eventual collapse of the Mafia and the nostalgic reaction that it induces has been portrayed excellently on screen by Martin Scorsese in both 1990's *Goodfellas* and 1995's *Casino*. The 1990 film follows the story of real-life former Lucchese Family (one of New York City's Five Families—the film does not explicitly mention the

Luccheses, however) associate Henry Hill, who ended up turning witness and ratting out all of his closest friends, the people he had looked up to and tried to emulate since childhood. *Goodfellas* portrays the perceived romanticism of Mob life, the yearning to become a "respected" made guy, and the eventual downfall of the Mafia due to a combination of drug dealing (and using), RICO suits, and the deterioration of "old school" Mafia principles. The film concludes with a seemingly depressed Henry Hill who, after contributing to the decimation of his own Family's ranks, laments at the fact that he must now live under witness protection, assuming a life of an average citizen, devoid of the thrill of being a "wise guy." For a guy like Henry Hill though, it was probably the best outcome he could have hoped for. The days when it was normal for mobsters to simply retire in their old age and live out their days in the spoils of their criminal career were over. In Hill's era, the life of nearly every mafioso ended in one of just a few predictable ways: you were shot by your enemies, shot by your friends, put in prison, or put in witness protection after betraying the trust of your colleagues.

The 1995 *Casino* also depicts in its closing moments the fading out of the Mafia's national power. Based on the Mafia's involvement in the gambling industry in Las Vegas, Nevada, *Casino* shows the national reach of the Mafia and exorbitant amounts of illicit income that the Families were once capable of "earning." The most powerful of the East Coast families had sent out their top made guys and associates to oversee the operations of casino establishments worth hundreds of millions of dollars, from which stacks of cash were routinely skimmed and sent back to New York City. The Patriarca Family was also involved in the casino business, particularly under Raymond Sr. In this case, his connections were very far-reaching—the vicious and infamous dictator of Haiti,

Francois Duvalier, was apparently a partner of Raymond's in the gambling industry. Duvalier welcomed organized crime in his brutalized nation and jumped at the opportunity to ally with someone as powerful as the Patriarca boss. When Raymond was facing the threat of prison time under his several indictments, Duvalier actually offered Raymond a home on his island. It's not clear how active the Patriarcas were in Nevada, though. *Casino* shows an era where the Mafia essentially ran the entire city of Las Vegas, had deep political connections with the city and state's administration, and where running afoul in one of their casinos typically meant a horrific beating rather than a ban. It was, to be sure, a far more violent period, but in the Mafia world it represented (and still represents) an ideal that is simply impossible to obtain in the 21st century. The closing of the film, similar to *Goodfellas*, pines for the loss of the Mafia's influence and expresses regret at the corporatization of Las Vegas (and to a lesser extent, Reno and Atlantic City, New Jersey) which has morphed it from an organized crime paradise to a family-friendly resort town.

Even the era when the American Mafia was crumbling under the weight of the FBI's intense scrutiny and the loss of Mafia principles has attracted critical acclaim and popular attention. The incredibly popular television series *The Sopranos*, which does a masterful job of portraying this period, is a perfect case in point. The lead character, Tony Soprano, is a man dealing with the loss of power and respect that came with the Mafia's severe downturn in the late 1990s and early 2000s. This, combined with various complications with his Family, has led him to seek psychiatric counseling, during which he exposes his deep longing for the days when mobsters like his father had it all, and everything seemed easier. Now as a Mafia boss operating during the turn of the century, he is head of an organization that had been eating itself alive for years. With little integrity, no honor, and an eagerness to avoid consequences by ratting out their friends, Tony Soprano is dissatisfied with his colleagues who comprise his Family. In the very first episode of the series, Tony perfectly sums up the anxiety related to the days when the end of the Mafia entirely seemed to be in sight: "I'd been thinking. It's good to be in something from the ground floor. I came too late for that, I know. But lately, I'm getting the feeling that I came in at the end. That the best is over," (Chase, January 10, 1999).

Indeed, the best was very much over. The once-mighty Patriarca clan has been reduced to a husk, one which used to embody the most powerful aspects of organized crime in America. An old Family dating all the way back to at least Gaspare Messina, the Patriarcas had staged a meteoric rise through the American underworld from the 1930s through to the 1960s and early 1970s and were helmed by one of the most powerful bosses in Mafia history for years. Extending its branches across state borders, the Patriarcas came to dominate Massachusetts and Rhode Island and penetrate the underworlds of other eastern states from Connecticut to Maine in the far northeast. Managing to secure their territory for decades from the other power and money-hungry Families, the strength of the Patriarcas rivaled even that of the legendary Genovese and Gambino Families to their west. As the decades wore on, internal struggles and rival ethnic gangs, particularly the Winter Hill Gang of Boston, became the biggest threat to the Patriarcas. Though the Family has seemingly recovered somewhat from the brink of dissolving entirely years ago, it remains a highly tenuous organization.

Today, most of the ranks of the Patriarca Family remain a mystery outside of speculation. This is expected, as the inherent secrecy of the Mafia means that the general public typically only learns the truth about events years, even decades, after the fact. That being said, it is generally assumed that Carmen "Cheese Man" Dinunzio, the elder of the DiNunzio brothers, remains boss of the Family to this day. DiNunzio has long been based out of Boston, so if he truly is the current boss this means their base of power remains in Massachusetts. As far as the public is aware, Eddie Lato also remains underboss in Providence. Clearly, then, the Patriarca Family is still a multi-state organization with influence across the seaboard. Guglielmetti, though he has taken a backseat in leadership, is still believed to be active in Rhode Island functioning as a regional captain. He also appears to have formed connections with the Philadelphia-based Bruno-Scarfo Family out of Pennsylvania. Joe Achille, the former *consigliere*, died in 2018 and it's not known who (if anyone) was chosen to replace him as top Family advisor. Costa and Ferrara appear to remain active in the Boston faction, as well as Freddie Simone and Carmen's younger brother and nephew, Anthony (released from prison in 2017) and Louis DiNunzio. Even less is known about the Providence faction ranks, which have likely been weakened as a result of the shift of main operations from Rhode Island to Massachusetts. Connecticut is even more obscure, but it is known that former Hartford underboss Will Grasso's son was involved in the Family's activities at least into the mid-2000s.

Overall, it is difficult to see any faction of the American Mafia, whether in Boston, New York City, Buffalo, or Los Angeles, ever returning to the criminal heyday that has been immortalized in productions like *Goodfellas* and *The Godfather*. Clearly, it is much more difficult to be a mobster these days, as RICO suits are an ever-present threat that could feasibly cripple an entire crew in one fell swoop. Further, there seems to be almost no semblance of the camaraderie and loyalty that once characterized the Mafia. As Songini explained, as far back as the bombshell Barboza testimonies, "the entire organization was eroding with mistrust—its edge was gone," (2015). Mafia Families are unlikely to dominate entire cities ever again, but that is not to say it is not a sometimes lucrative business. Well into the 21st century, the Sicilian-American organization remains active and they continue in most of their old rackets, though some have become infeasible. Corporatization has rendered the practice of extortion a mostly pointless endeavor, but prostitution, loan sharking, and drug smuggling remain typical. There is still plenty of room for organized criminals to build illicit empires, but these days it seems that it always leads to prison.

REFERENCES

Barry, S. (2011, December 11). *Organized crime in Springfield evolved through death and money.* Mass Live.

https://www.masslive.com/news/2011/12/organized_crime_in_springfield.html

Carr, H. (2007, October 14). *Mobster of the week: Joseph "J.R." Russo.* Boston Herald.

Chase, D. (writer & director). (1999, January 10). Pilot episode (Season 1, episode 1).

In Chase, D. (execute producer) *The Sopranos.* HBO.

Critchley, D. (2009). *The origins of organized crime in America: The New York City*

Mafia, 1891-1931. New York City: Routledge.

Estate of Iaconi v. Commissioner (1961, April 13). Leagle.com

https://www.leagle.com/decision/196152220cztcm5021419

Foderaro, L. (1989, June 18). Mob leader's slaying may signal power struggle. *New York Times.*

Ford, B. & Schorow, S. (2011). *The Boston mob guide: Hitmen, hoodlums & hideouts.*

Charleston, North Carolina: The History Press.

Frankfurter, F. (1927, March). *The case of Sacco and Vanzetti*. The Atlantic. https://www.theatlantic.com/magazine/archive/1927/03/the-case-of-sacco-and-vanzetti/306625/

Jacobs, J. & Gouldin, L. (1999). Cosa nostra: The final chapter? *Crime and Justice* 25, 129-189.

Maher, S. (2009, February 17). *The Worcester mafia and gambling*. InCity Times. https://archive.ph/20131003040242/http://incitytimesworcester.org/2009/02/17/the-worcester-mafia-and-gambling/%23more-859

Meyer, P. (2015). Going beyond the evidence: A skilled trial lawyer uses narrative persuasion to deliver a story to the jury in a complex criminal case. *ABA Journal* 101(2), 26-27.

New York Times (1980, December 6). Patriarca, crime figure, charged as an accessory to 1965 slaying.

New England Patriarca Crime Leaders (n.d.). Mafia History. https://mafiahistory.us/maf-b-ne.html

Peter Limone (n.d.). The National Registry of Exonerations. https://www.law.umich.edu/special/exoneration/Pages/casedetail.aspx?caseid=3383

Senate.gov

Smith, G. (2013, December 11). *City orders Satin Doll closed for 20 days, proposes new limits on strip clubs*. The Providence Journal. https://www.providencejournal.com/story/news/crime/2013/12/11/20131211-city-orders-satin-doll-closed-asks-for-new-limits-on-operation-of-strip-clubs-ece/35380370007/

Songini, M. (2015). *Boston mob: The rise and fall of the New England mob and its most notorious killer.* New York City: St. Martin's Press.

Telford, T. (2018, September 14). *Boston mobster known as 'cadillac Frank' gets life in prison for an old murder.* The Washington Post.

https://www.washingtonpost.com/crime-law/2018/09/14/long-dark-chapter-ends-boston-mobster-known-cadillac-gets-life-prison-murder/

White, T. (2023, July 13). *Mobster Joe DeLuca, who testified against former mafia kingpin, has died.* WPRI.com

https://www.wpri.com/target-12/inside-the-mafia/mobster-joe-deluca-who-testified-against-former-mafia-kingpin-has-died/

Made in United States
North Haven, CT
05 July 2025